George Washington Carver had a special prayer which he repeated for all the people he knew as well as for the many strangers the Lord would bring into his life:

> *May God ever bless, keep, guide, and continue to prosper you in your uplifting work for humanity, be it great or small, is my prayer. And may those whom He has redeemed learn to walk and talk with Him, not only daily and hourly, but momently, through the things that He has created.*

Born to slave parents, young George was orphaned before he could walk. In his youth he fought poverty and throughout his life he battled prejudice. Yet George Washington Carver emerges as one of history's most remarkable men!

How?

"The Lord has guided me," Carver was often heard to say. "He has shown me the way, just as He will show everyone who turns to Him."

This book is written as George Washington Carver might have told the story of his life. Hopefully you will experience his joys, sorrows, anxieties, and zeal for learning of God's creation with him.

"Without my Savior, I am nothing," declared Carver.

With his Savior, the Lord Jesus Christ, George Washington Carver was greatly used by God to discover countless numbers of scientific wonders and to lead a life which has inspired millions of Christians everywhere!

This volume of *George Washington Carver: Man's Slave Becomes God's Scientist* joins a collecting of inspiring biographies written by one of America's foremost authors of childrens literature—David R. Collins.

Among his other works are: *Abraham Lincoln: God's Leader for a Nation*, *Francis Scott Key: God's Courageous Composer*, *Johnny Appleseed: John Chapman, God's Faithful Planter*, *Florence Nightingale: God's Servant at the Battlefield*, and *Noah Webster: Master of Words*.

"I choose subjects who have had a strong Christian influence in their lives," states Collins. "This influence led them to serve other people and make a better world for all of us."

David R. Collins is an English instructor at Woodrow Wilson Junior High School in Moline, Illinois. He earned his Bachelor of Science and Master of Science degrees from Western Illinois University.

In 1975, David Collins was named "Outstanding Educator" by the Illinois Office of Education.

In Moline, Collins maintains a busy schedule of church, civic and educational activities. He is a popular speaker and frequently appears at national writers conferences.

George Washington Carver

MAN'S SLAVE BECOMES GOD'S SCIENTIST

By

DAVID R. COLLINS

Illustrated by **Joe Van Severen**

MOTT MEDIA

Fenton, Michigan 48430

Dedication
This book is for Susan,
with affection and admiration.

Robert F. Burkett, Editor

LIBRARY OF CONGRESS CATALOGING IN PUBLICATION DATA

Collins, David R.
    George Washington Carver, Man's Slave Becomes God's Scientist

    (The Sowers)
    Bibliography: p. 131
    Includes index.

    SUMMARY: George Washington Carver recounts the story of his life and shares his faith and dependence upon his Savior, Jesus Christ.
        1. Carver, George Washington, 18 -1943—Juvenile literature, Biography. 2. Science. 3. Faith. I. VanSeveren, Joe. II. Title.

Library of Congress No. 81-86454
ISBN-10: 0-915134-90-X Paperbound
ISBN-13: 978-0-915134-90-8

CONTENTS

Death in the Trees

I had never seen anything so ugly and frightening. Death hung there in the trees. Ugly brown death.

I don't know what made me look up to see it. Maybe it was the whisper of the wind from the nearby Ozark Hills. Maybe it was the lark's happy song—or a thrush calling to her children.

No, I don't think it was any of those sounds. Those were the Missouri sounds I heard every day.

This sound was different. It seemed to come from inside me. It was like an echo of the words Master Carver had said that morning from the Psalms.

"Lift up thine eyes!" echoed the voice within me. "Lift up thine eyes!"

Master Carver had closed the big black Bible in front of him. Slowly he stood up and left the room. His wife, Frau Carver, and I sat looking at each other. Finally she smiled.

"You like the words of the Lord, don't you, George?" she said softly.

I stood up and walked to the big black Book on the

kitchen table. Yes, I did like those words. Carefully I ran my fingers along the letters printed deep in the book's cover—HOLY BIBLE.

Frau Carver arose and walked to stand beside me. She rested her hand on my shoulder. "If only you might share your own words with us, boy. If only we knew your thoughts and feelings. Just try to talk. Open your mouth and speak—"

Master Carver appeared at the doorway. "Come, boy. There's a cow to milk, hogs to feed, rakin' to be done in the orchard."

Quickly I ran outside not wanting Master Carver to become angry. He was a hard worker, and he expected everyone in his house to be the same.

I was happy when my chores around the barn were finished. The air near the barn was heavy—too stale and closed-in.

Raking in the orchard was a far more happy task. There a person could smell the apple blossoms and listen to the birds singing. After the early morning rains, I liked to pick up handfuls of dirt. The rich darkness of the soil blended with my own black skin. It made me feel a part of the world—alive and good.

"Lift up thine eyes!"

It was then the words had rumbled inside me. I looked up. There, on a distant limb, was an ugly patch of brown. It ruined the thick blanket of green, the growing blossoms and leaves. Death. Yes, death was growing on that branch. It was spreading, reaching out to kill and leave behind its ugliness. My thin body shook with fear. I had to find Master Carver.

Quickly I dashed to the barn. Master Carver was just opening the barn door to bring out the horse. I grabbed his sleeve and pulled.

"What is it, boy? I have work to do."

Again I tugged, this time harder. But the tall man

jerked his arm away. How I wanted to speak, but the words would not come.

"Get back to work, boy!" he ordered. "You'll not be getting supper if your work is not done. Go now—and let me be!"

I dropped my hand to my side. I knew well Master Carver's voice. He was finished talking. He would not come and look at the death in the tree.

A new thought came to me. I raced back to the orchard. Quickly I found a stone in the pile I had raked. With as much strength as I could, I hurled it at the dead limb.

The stone fell short. Not wasting a moment, I found another in the pile. Again I sailed it skyward.

Crack!

The stone found its mark. A brown leaf dropped off the dead limb and floated downward. I grabbed it from the ground below. Just as I thought, the leaf was covered with tiny bugs. They had killed this leaf—and there were hundreds, maybe millions more, spreading death. Quickly I ran to find Master Carver.

He was mending a fence near the barn. Pulling at his sleeve with one hand, I held out the leaf with the other.

"Boy, let go of me. Stop your foolish playing. I've got no time for you now."

I *had* to make him listen, to see the death in the tree. Once more I pulled his arm. "C-come."

Master Carver spun around. "So, I get a whole word from you, do I? One whole word. At least you prove you are not a complete mute. But a word is not enough, boy. Go on with you."

My heart pounded. I longed to tell the master of the evil in the tree—the death killing the leaves. But the words would not spill out. I choked, my throat full of strange noises. But no words.

I stepped back from Master Carver. I raced to the

house, leaping the porch stairs two at a time. Frau Carver was kneading bread. She looked up as the back door banged open.

"George, what makes you run so fast?" A cloud of flour rose as she rubbed her hands together.

I held out my hand to show her the leaf. "D-dead," I stuttered. "D-d-death in t-tree."

Frau Carver raised her apron to wipe away the sweat from her head. "A dead weed, is it?" The woman nodded, then continued to pound the dough on the table. "That is good, George. Take it outside and throw it away."

I shook my head. Again I pushed the leaf forward. Frau Carver frowned.

"Yes, I saw it. Did you not hear me, George? I see what you are holding. Take it outside and throw it away."

It was hopeless. No one could see the death. I dashed out the door and threw the leaf into the wind. It tossed in the Missouri breeze.

After supper that night I did not want to listen to Master Carver read from the big black Bible. Quickly I tried to slip away.

"Where are you going, boy?" Master Carver's voice sounded harsh. "We have not yet heard our Father's words."

I sat down on the floor by the door. Master sat in his big chair while Frau Carver sat on a small bench by the wall. As Master read, my mind traveled to the orchard where the bugs were eating away the leaves. I heard Master Carver talk about the effect of "sins on the soul." Were not the deadly bugs like sins too? Should they not be killed before they spread?

I squirmed and wiggled on the floor. The song of night crickets grew louder.

Master Carver closed the big black Book. "You are not a good listener tonight, boy. It is sad you will share so few words of your own and yet will not listen to the wise and good words of the Father. Off to bed with you."

Sadly I left the room. In my bed I lay awake thinking. I was sorry I had angered Master Carver. But it was he who had read, "Lift up thine eyes." I had done that and I had seen the death in the tree. Why couldn't Master Carver see it, too?

"Our Father's words." How often Master Carver spoke of "our Father's words." I knew it was not my real father the master talked about.

My real father was dead. "A good hard worker he was," Master Carver said often. "A man of muscle and power. Fell off a team of oxen and got trampled to death."

I don't ever remember seeing my father. I can't really remember my mother either. But the story Frau Carver often told me brought back thoughts of my mother.

"She was a good woman, boy. She loved you so much. One night those awful riders came. They were a fearful pack of thieves, always looking for slaves to steal from homes. Those night riders took you and your mother. Left your poor sister dead."

Frau Carver stopped a moment. She dabbed at her eyes with a handkerchief. "Master Carver stayed here to look after me. But some of the other menfolk from over the hill at Diamond Grove took off after those night riders. Master Carver sent his best horse with the men from Diamond Grove. He told them to trade the horse for you and your mother."

A horse for my mother and me. It was kind of Master Carver, for his horse was always needed for farm work.

"The men from Diamond Grove caught up with the night riders. The thieves agreed to trade. They told the men from Diamond Grove to tie the horse to a tree and

leave. They did as the riders said, but those awful men rode off with the horse and your poor mother. Only you were left, George, wrapped in a torn damp blanket. You were a tiny sick babe, scarcely six months old. Only the good Lord knows where your mother is now. Sometimes I think she is with Him already. Mary was a fine woman. I was glad enough to take you in for her sake."

I was grateful to Master Carver and his wife for their kindness. I only wished I might have been more help to them, but my body was skinny and small. If only my arms and legs would grow thick and firm like the Master's. I wished I could have the strength of my older brother, Jim. He cared little for the farm. Jim chose to wander about the countryside by himself. His body, with its hard muscles, could have done much for Master Carver on the farm. But it was not Jim's wish to work by plowing and harvesting for the Carvers.

Some people said I had no folks. Master Carver never let such a statement go by without argument.

"He's got us, the wife and me, to give him food and a home on this earth," the Master would say. "And he's got the same loving Father who tends all of us in His flock. The boy's been made by God, like us all. The wife and me will see the boy receives Christ as his Savior and trusts in Him for salvation."

I liked to hear Master Carver talk like that. It made me feel good inside. I felt the same way when I heard the words from the big black Bible. The words made me feel safe and strong.

But that morning the big black Book had said to "Lift up thine eyes." Why did Master Carver read those words, yet not obey them? If he had but seen the death in the tree . . .

Early the next morning in the misty darkness I slid from my bed and dressed silently. The saw hung in its place in the barn. I took it down and hurried to the tree of death.

I slid the saw around my shoulder and climbed upward. It was no easy task. Finally I reached the bad limb and began sawing it off.

A squirrel scolded me from a nearby branch. The thrushes sang their early morning songs. I wondered if they were singing about me.

Up and down I pulled the saw. My tired hands felt raw and sweaty. Up and down. Back and forth. Slowly the limb cracked and bent downward.

"You, boy! Get down from there. Dummkopf! You are ruining the tree!"

Master Carver stood on the ground below. His face blazed red as he shook his fist. It was the same way he shook it at the black crows in the garden.

But I had to finish. The sweat stung my eyes as I kept sawing. My heart pounded louder and louder. Just a few more strokes and . . .

"Fool! Stop that at once! Have you lost your senses?"

Master Carver moved to the bottom of the tree and began shaking it. Angry German words filled the air. He could think and speak faster in the language from his native Germany.

Finally, the dead limb broke off and fell to the ground in a dull thud. Gone. The ugly brown death lay at Master Carver's feet. After dropping the saw, I slid down the tree as fast as I could.

Master Carver grabbed me from the tree before I reached the ground. He shook me from side to side.

"Dummkopf! You are worthless!" he shouted.

Suddenly Frau Carver pulled him away. Once free, I ran to the dead limb on the ground. I broke off a cluster of dead leaves and ran to Frau Carver.

"B-bad!" I stuttered. "D-d-death!"

I could not say more. The words would not come. They caught in my throat. Frau Carver took the branch and looked at it closely.

"Why, this is covered with bugs!" she exclaimed. "The bugs have killed all the leaves. They might have killed the whole tree, the whole orchard."

I nodded, wiping away the tears from my cheeks. Master Carver stepped closer and took the dead branch. He looked confused.

"But—but I have worked out here each day," he mumbled. "I saw no bugs. How could the boy have seen them?"

Frau Carver pulled me close to her. She patted my back and hugged me.

"The boy sees things we do not," she answered softly. "I cannot grow flowers in the garden. The boy can. He is a friend to the birds and animals. He talks to them, sings with them."

Master Carver said nothing. He kept looking at the dead leaves.

"We are all children made by God," Frau Carver

said, kneeling down to me. "But you, George, are one of
His special children."

A Quiet Voice

Master Carver treated me more kindly after that day in the orchard. Frau Carver did, too. She taught me how to bake biscuits and corn bread. I liked to sit on the back porch and churn the butter, too.

One night Frau Carver and I fixed a grand dinner for the Master. "This fried chicken is the best I've ever tasted!" he exclaimed, taking a giant bite. "I'm happy I have such a fine cook in my kitchen."

Frau Carver smiled. "Your cook had a most able helper," she said.

Master Carver looked at me and nodded. The meat on the chicken leg he held disappeared rapidly into his mouth.

Frau Carver reached over and rubbed her hand softly over my curly hair. "I think it is time our George had a full name. Why, it is 1874, and the boy is at least ten years old."

No answer came from Master Carver. He still

nibbled away at the last pieces of meat on the chicken leg.

"I think George Washington Carver would be most suitable," Frau Carver continued. She arose from the table and sat down near the cabin fireplace. From a basket next to her rocking chair, she took out one of Master's shirts.

Master Carver pushed his chair back from the table. "George Washington Carver," he repeated. "That sounds a mite fancy. We called the boy George after his Pa. That seemed a bit foolish. His Pa was a chunk of muscle and strength, while the boy has always been skinny and frail. I've no quarrel with callin' the boy Carver. These slave children must have a last name now that they're free. But Washington . . . "

All this talk got me mighty excited. No longer could I sit quietly at the table. I slipped off my chair and took a place on the old wooden stool by the fireplace. Drawing my bony knees up under my chin, I looked over at Frau Carver. I hoped she would not give up. "George Washington Carver" had a fine sound to it. Maybe it was fancy, but I liked it.

Frau Carver was mending one of Master's shirts. For several minutes her hands flew silently over the cloth.

"Yes," she said finally. "George Washington Carver it will be. The George in honor of his poor dead Pa, the Carver for us who have raised him. And Washington, well, because it fits the boy's character. The lad is willing to work even when the task is a big one. And the child is honest. Moses Carver, you've got to admit that. The boy *is* honest."

Master Carver only grunted. It was not an accepting

grunt, so Frau Carver knew she had more convincing to do.

"Remember last week when you told George to chop the wood by the shed?"

I shook my head, wishing Frau Carver had not mentioned that day. It was the day I had gone to care for my baby fish. I had put them into a fish house until they could care for themselves. When I went to free them I'd forgotten all about chopping the wood as the Master had told me.

"I remember it well," Master Carver answered. "The wood was not chopped when I wanted it. The boy forgot his work. Is that why we should call him Washington?"

Frau Carver shook her head. "No, it is because he did not lie or make excuses. He never has lied to us, even when a whipping was coming. That is what was said about the first George Washington, too."

Again Master Carver grunted. But this time I knew he agreed. My name was to be George Washington Carver. I prayed to the Lord that I might bring honor to such a fine name.

I was glad I had a name in the days that followed. My older brother Jim came to me one morning. He said he was leaving and would not be back. Although we had spent little time together as brothers, I felt an emptiness inside.

"We ain't slaves no more," Jim told me. "We can go where we want and do what we want. I ain't goin' to stay around here hirin' out and workin' the fields. There's a lot more to this world than these Ozark Hills and the state of Missouri. I'm goin' to see some."

Leaving sounded exciting, like an adventure, the way

Jim talked. But somehow I knew it couldn't be all good. Anyway, I was happy with the Carvers—too happy to leave.

Together Jim and I walked to the edge of the farm where our little sister lay buried. The wet dew felt cool under our bare feet. The tiny grave lay covered by bright colored stones and green moss. Jim and I stood silently, sharing prayers to the Lord.

After Jim was gone, I spent more and more time in my own special place. It was a garden not far from the cabin. Everything seemed to grow there—flowers, plants, and animals. One time I found a baby bird that looked almost dead. I took the bird to my garden. Each day I brought it fresh water and bits of dry bread. Before long, my friend was dipping and diving in the wind.

One hot, sultry afternoon a woman came to visit

Frau Carver. Her name was Mrs. Mueller. She was tall and wore a bright calico dress. I was weeding the rose bushes by the front porch when Frau Carver and Mrs. Mueller came outside. Right away I smelled the visitor's perfume. Her lilac scent mingled with the scent of the roses.

"George, Mrs. Mueller wants you to come over to her house," said Frau Carver. "I've told her you would help her with her plants."

I smiled and nodded eagerly. I liked working with plants and flowers. The Lord planted the seeds and I helped them grow. He guided my hands and showed me what to do.

"I've got something for you," Mrs. Mueller said one morning after I had finished working. She handed me a thick blue book. "This is a speller, George. It's a book filled with words, words for you to learn. Just as you have learned about nature, you should also learn to read, to write, and to speak the words in this book."

I took the book, nodding my thanks. I turned the book over and over in my hands. It was mine, my own book. I had never had a book of my own. The pages were clean and unwrinkled. They felt smooth and clean. Quickly I hurried home to show Frau Carver. She had helped me learn words from the big black Bible. Maybe I could learn the words in this book, too.

I kept the speller in my special garden. Sometimes I took it to the cabin. Both Frau and Master Carver helped me learn the letters and words.

"This word is 'smile,' George," Frau Carver told me, pointing to a word on the page. "It's the way your mouth looks when you're happy."

"S-sm-ile," I repeated. "S-smile. Smile."

Frau Carver laughed, "Yes, George. Yes."

One night we rode a buggy over to the next farm. Master Herman Jaeger lived there. He was a small man, stout and firm. His eyes sparkled, like they held happy secrets and much wisdom. A thick pile of whiskers covered half his face. I listened proudly as Master Carver said good things about me.

"The boy is only ten," he said, "but he has a way about him. He never forgets a word. Can write them, too. Knows every flower and plant on my farm."

"If he is as able in the classroom as he is on your farm, he should be in school." Farmer Jaeger smiled at me, stroking his grey whiskers. "There is a school for colored children in Neosho. The boy might do right well there."

Master Carver looked at me. "But the boy seldom speaks. He listens well, but says little."

Farmer Jaeger nodded, slipping his thumbs inside his suspenders and stretching them. "Remember James 1:19 from the Bible, my friend? 'Let every man be swift to hear, slow to speak, slow to wrath.' This lad seems to show wisdom beyond his young years."

I liked Farmer Jaeger. His words sounded strong, like the words in the big black Book.

As we rode back to the cabin that night, I thought about the school in Neosho. I wondered if the Master would let me go. One thing was certain. If he agreed, I was willing.

Off to Neosho

"My, you do look handsome. Turn around, George."

Frau Carver tugged on the coat she had made me. Master Carver watched from the doorway, framed by a bright autumn sunset.

I looked down at my feet. How I hated wearing the stiff new shoes Mrs. Mueller had given me. They pinched my toes.

"The boy should wear shoes to school in Neosho," Mrs. Mueller had said. "This pair belonged to my nephew, but he seldom wore them."

It was a kind gift. Yet I knew why Mrs. Mueller's nephew seldom wore the hard shoes. How could trapped toes feel the fresh cool dew on the grass? How could a person wearing shoes wade in the pond and sink into the mud along the shore?

The shoes were not the only gift Mrs. Mueller had given me. Carefully she had taken a whole handful of coins and tied them in the corner of a handkerchief.

When Frau Carver and I counted them, we found they added up to a full dollar. Never had I felt so many coins. Again and again I jingled them in my cupped hands. The coins made a wonderful sound!

"It's the least I can give you for your hard work," Mrs. Mueller had said. "You turned my tiny garden into a paradise. Surely the Lord guides your hands."

I *was* a mite proud of the work I had done for Mrs. Mueller. Bright red and yellow roses climbed the white trellis and fence. Patches of daisies and iris trimmed the pathways. Giant purple lilac spears hung from huge bushes. The smell of the garden was sweeter than all of Mrs. Mueller's perfumes.

"Now, I think you are ready for school," Frau Carver said. "Take care with the shawl that holds your things. It will be a warm cover on cold nights this fall."

I took the bag that Frau Carver had packed. It was full of bumps and bulges. Inside was my spelling book, my best knife for trimming plants, two apples from the orchard, and a sandwich. With the money in my pocket, I felt awful important. I only wished the shoes would stop pinching my toes.

"Sorry I can't be taking you to Neosho in the cart." Master Carver shoved his hands deep into his pockets. "But there's a sick calf in the barn that needs tending."

"It's all r-r-right," I answered. "I know the w-w-way."

I made my good-byes as swiftly as I could. Master Carver shook my hand, just like he always shook Farmer Jaeger's. But I was glad the Master pulled me to him for a strong hug. I felt older, maybe a bit too important, but that hug felt awful good.

Frau Carver fell to her knees and pulled me to her. I felt the wetness of her tears against my head.

"S-smile," I reminded her. I moved my fingers around her lips, wiping away the frown and tracing instead a smile. Frau Carver nodded, blinking away the sadness in her eyes.

"Now, when you get to Neosho, you go to the big houses," Frau Carver ordered. "Tell people you are a good worker. Tell them you can plant seeds, pull weeds, milk cows, pick crops— everything you've done here. Ask them only for a few bites of food for pay. Maybe you can find a barn to sleep in, or an empty shed."

I fumbled with the bag I held. "Yes, ma'am."

"Just don't let folks treat you like a slave, George," warned Master Carver. "Those days are past."

Minutes later I hurried away from the cabin. I did not look back. The sight of Master and Frau Carver might have stopped me from going.

I knew I would miss Mrs. Mueller, the flowers, AND my friends in the orchard and woods. But strangely enough at ten years old and out on my own I did not feel alone. The good Lord had said in Exodus 23:20, "Behold, I send an Angel before thee, to keep thee in the way." As I walked the eight miles to Neosho, more words from the big black Bible pounded into my mind— Zephaniah 3:12, "Trust in the name of the Lord." The Lord had said in Matthew 28:20, "Lo, I am with you alway." I *did* trust, and I felt safe.

Soon I stopped along the road. I wasted no time in slipping off those awful shoes. Again my toes breathed fresh air. I tied the strings of the shoes together and looped them over my neck. The dust of the road felt good under my feet.

It was dark by the time I reached Neosho. The Master and I had visited the town often, but never at night. I found a quiet barn not far from the flour mill. No sooner had I fallen into a pile of hay when I heard a frightening sound.

"Gr-r-r-." Two gold spots sparkled in the dark.

My eyes widened to make out the form of a large dog at my feet. His glowing eyes were big, too, and he kept up his steady mean growl.

What to do? My stomach rolled and tossed inside. But suddenly the answer came to me. Did the Lord not meet enemies with kindness?

"Easy, e-easy, boy," I whispered. "Let us b-b-be f-f-friends."

Carefully I moved forward. I lifted my right arm slowly, softly stroking the dog's head and back. In moments my new friend was licking my face. When I lay back again, the dog snuggled close to me. Sleep came within minutes.

My dog friend had disappeared by morning. Maybe he had gone to seek a bone or table scraps. Such thoughts reminded me of the rumbling within my own stomach. The food Frau Carver had sent with me had been eaten along the road to Neosho.

I scrambled down from the loft and out into the cool morning air. A breeze stung my cheeks, causing me to pull the shawl around my shoulders. I felt the money and knife in my pockets, and my shoes hung around my neck.

Remembering a livery stable not far away, I hastened my steps. A tall man wearing a widebrimmed cowboy hat was just pushing open the heavy doors to his barn.

"N-Need help, Mister?" I asked. "I-I can rub down y-y-your horses, water 'em an' clean the stalls."

The man tugged at one suspender and looked at me closely. "And what be your price, black boy?"

"A b-bite or two of b-breakfast?"

The man turned. "Come on with you then. I've a biscuit or two. They're hard, mind you, from being left out. But you can soften 'em with my boiling coffee." I could smell the brew's strong odor in the air.

The man had spoken true, both about the biscuits and coffee. I do believe there were softer stones around the Carver's cabin, and the coffee burned the skin off my tongue.

For the food the man supplied, I worked two hours in the stable. Then I slipped into my shoes, brushed off my pants and coat, and headed for the schoolhouse.

I hoped I was not late. But my hopes were lost. As I pulled open the wooden door to the one room building, a sad creak announced my entry. Pairs of eyes looked at me from every side as I walked up to the schoolmaster's desk at the front of the room.

The whispers in the building were loud and echoed. "Look at that dirty one!" a muscular boy said. "He's got straw in his hair. Must sleep with the horses."

There was no time to stop. I faced the teacher, a man with light brown skin. "Almost don't look like a black," Master Carver might have said.

"And what is your name?" the schoolmaster said, his voice revealing anger at having to stop a lesson.

"My name is—is George Washington Carver." I was proud my voice sounded steady and firm, but still I heard laughter behind me.

The tall schoolmaster took a ruler into his hand. He began slapping it against one of his palms.

"I-I have money," I said quickly. "Here, it's for school . . . from Mrs. Mueller."

As the knotted handkerchief filled with coins dropped on his desk, the schoolmaster continued watching me. My face and hands felt sweaty. I wanted to run out of the building.

"You may find a seat, my half-witted friend, and maybe we will let you stay." The schoolmaster motioned with the ruler for me to sit down.

I backed away, finding an empty stool away from the others in the room. As the hours ticked away, the schoolmaster read aloud. There were problems with numbers and a story about a pirate ship. The numbers left me confused. But the story was a joyful tale about a great sea battle.

Finally, the schoolmaster said, "Dismissed." It was a strange word to me, but the other boys and girls arose and left. I did not know where to go.

"You! Half-wit! Run along home!"

Again the schoolmaster had called me by a name not my own. I stood and looked at him. "My name is George Washington Carver."

The schoolmaster pushed back his chair and smiled. "Well, my friend with hair of hay, tomorrow you shall be here on time, clean, and a bit more mannerly. Now run along home."

Home. Where was home? As I left the schoolhouse, I knew but one home in Neosho. I hoped the hayloft would be warm during the winter months. Hopefully too, the people of Neosho would offer work to me. Surely there were those who would let me cut their wood, run errands, rub down their horses, and rake their yards.

Soon I would find out.

Each day when I lived with the Carvers I had prayed to the Lord. He had always taken care of me.

"I need You now even more," I whispered into the wind as I walked along. "Please stay with me and help me. Without You, Lord, I am nothing—nothing at all."

A New Home

All eyes in the classroom were watching me. I took a deep breath and recited the final words of President Lincoln's "Gettysburg Address":

> *. . . that this nation, under God, shall have a new birth of freedom—and that, government of the people, by the people, for the people, shall not perish from the earth.*

Proudly I sat back down on my stool. I was finally beginning to overcome my habit of stuttering. There were no sounds in the room. Finally, the boy next to me leaned over.

"That was good, George," he whispered. "Those were good words, and you said them good, too."

I sat facing the schoolmaster. How I wished he would say something. For days I had worked on my recitation. There had been no mistakes. But somehow I knew the schoolmaster would find fault.

"Well, I've heard a lot better," he said, slowly pulling his right ear. "And I've heard a lot worse. You surely don't have the best voice to listen to, Master Carver."

For a moment I squirmed on my stool. I knew my voice was high and squeaky. How I wished the schoolmaster—then suddenly his words echoed in my head. "Master Carver—Master Carver." For the first time, he had not called me "Half-wit." Joy filled my whole body.

"Thank you, Lord, for helping me," I murmured to myself.

The schoolmaster rose. "Class is dismissed," he announced.

My classmates leaped from their stools and raced toward the door. I was among the leaders. The last one out was often assigned the chores of carrying in the wood for the stove and sweeping the floor. They were thankless tasks, often taking an hour, with the schoolmaster's stern stare always present. I needed to be off earning money for food.

Other places in Neosho offered happier opportunities for work. Each day after school I visited the rich families with the big houses. "Need any cleaning done?" I asked. "Want any errands run?"

Usually work was easy to find. People seemed willing to pay with food rather than money.

As fall slipped into winter, my home in the barn grew colder. The shawl sent from Frau Carver found a mate in a torn blanket left inside the barn door. Each night when I went to bed, I buried myself in the hay with the shawl and blanket wrapped around me. Such a strange sight probably scared off the mice and rats.

When the spring planting season arrived, the schoolmaster turned us loose. Everyone ran shouting, "No classes! No more studies!" There was much work to be done in the fields.

Wasting no time, I headed for the farm of Master Jaeger. He had promised me work when I needed it. But sad news awaited me when I arrived.

"The man's dead, boy," a stranger on the farm said. "He died this winter. He was an old man, you know."

The words left me with a feeling of emptiness. Farmer Jaeger had been a kind friend, a good and gentle person. He looked so big and strong. Only the thought of him enjoying the glory of heaven lessened the tears on my return to Neosho. The barn seemed especially cold and lonely that night. I decided I would return to the Carvers, hoping they would have work for me.

I was awakened the next morning by a boot prodding my side. Quickly I sat up and rubbed my eyes. High above me stood a white man, holding a fearful pitchfork. Was he going to jab me? My heart pounded.

"On your feet, boy!" The man's voice was sharp. "Who are you? What are you doing here?"

I scrambled to my feet, trying to untangle the shawl and blanket. Words stuck in my throat. I heard my heart pounding through my whole body.

"My—ah—my name is George—George Washington Carver." I swallowed deeply. "In the day I go to school. I-I just sleep here at night."

The stranger leaned the pitchfork against the barn wall. "You been sleepin' out here nights? Why, it's lucky you didn't freeze to death."

I nodded, remembering the mornings when I found myself with silvery frost on my toes, hands, and cheeks.

A smile crossed the man's face and he pulled me forward. "Come on, my friend. You look like you could use a bite to eat."

I was a mite skinny. My old pants grew more loose each week. Together we walked outside. The man cupped his hand around my shoulder.

"My name is John Martin," he said. "My wife is Lucy, and a better cook you'll not be finding in these parts."

Minutes later I sat eating hot beef stew in a warm kitchen. John Martin had spoken the truth about his wife.

"He's starving," I overheard Mrs. Martin whisper to her husband. "The poor little fellow. You can see his bones."

A visit with John Martin to a small shed behind the house followed my meal in the kitchen. The shed was a cheery place, with a chair and a cot. Two framed flower pictures hung on the walls.

"With some scrubbing and sweeping, this would be a sight better than the barn for sleepin' in," John Martin said. "You take to those tasks, and I'll see if I don't have some other clothes for you to wear."

It all seemed like a dream. Surely the Lord held me close that day. By the time I had finished cleaning the shed, John Martin had returned with a shirt and pants. Unlike my own, the clothes he brought had no holes.

Sleep came swiftly that night. I was grateful for that since I had special plans for the next morning.

Before the sun arose, I crept into the house. The Martin kitchen was similar to Frau Carver's. Quickly I busied myself, trying not to awaken anyone in the house.

Minutes later, the smell of hot coffee and golden wheat cakes drifted through the house. John and Lucy Martin appeared at the kitchen doorway.

"Well, jumpin' jack rabbits!" John exclaimed. "What's all this?"

I smiled, pulling out the wooden bench by the table. "It is breakfast," I answered. "But please sit down now while the wheat cakes are hot."

Lucy Martin gave a close inspection to the cakes on the stove. She seemed unable to believe what she saw. "But-but who taught you to do this?"

"Frau Carver," I said, pouring a mug full of coffee. "I can cook, wash, dust, and clean just about anything around the house."

John Martin nodded. "If your wheat cakes and coffee taste as good as they smell, I'm a mite glad you picked my barn for sleepin' in."

"That's the truth!" Lucy Martin laughed. "I think we'll just be keeping you around a while, George Washington Carver."

My heart pounded happily. I had earned myself a new home!

Little did I suspect that the Martins had plans for me as I worked in their garden one afternoon. It was a week after they had taken me in.

For a moment I stopped digging in the Martins' front yard. A light breeze carried the soft melody of a whippoorwill in the distance. The bird's song was a bit sad.

Looking up I gazed in wonder at the sunset. Streaks of deep purple and gold melted in the sky around the sun as it slipped silently behind the Ozark Hills. I recalled the words of Psalm 19:

The heavens declare the glory of God; and the firmament showeth His handiwork. Day unto day uttereth speech, and night unto night showeth knowledge. There is no speech nor language, where their voice is not heard. Their line is gone out through all the earth, and their words to the end of the world. In them hath he set a tabernacle for the sun.

Returning to my work, I shoveled a final mound of dirt around the small snowball bush I had just planted. If all went well, it would soon bear happy white puffs of flowers to cheer all who passed by.

Down the street came Mr. Martin. He worked as a foreman at the flour mill.

"So you got the bush planted!" he laughed. "And I bet the house is clean from any spot of dust."

I smiled and nodded. Such chores were little enough to do in return for the cot and food the Martins gave me.

"George, why don't you go play with the boys down

the street?" he asked, as he inspected the bush. "I'm not certain what game it is, but their shouts tell me they're having a grand time."

I shook my head. Games held little interest for me. There were too many important things to do.

But that night at the supper table, Mr. Martin had another thought. As he sipped his steaming coffee, he looked over at me and told me his plan.

"George, my wife and I think you should pay a visit to the church for coloreds over on the edge of town. There will be folks your own age and race there. You feel strongly toward the Lord. You may as well be praying in His house on Sundays."

I shook my head. "The whole world belongs to the Lord. I pray to Him in the woods, or outside on the porch, or in the shed . . ."

"Please, George," Mrs. Martin said, resting her hand on my arm. "The singing is so lovely in the church. I think you'd like it there."

I offered no more argument. The Martins had treated me kindly. It was a small request.

Early Sunday morning I scrubbed myself clean, then slipped into the plain shirt and pants Mrs. Martin had washed for me. Soon I was headed to church.

Other folks streamed up the stairs into the front church doors. Ladies wore fancy bonnets and dresses that swished. The menfolk looked right handsome in dark ties and coats. Still, I felt little shame in my old but clean clothes, for I knew the Lord cared nothing about how His people dressed to pray.

Silently I slipped into the back pew of the church. In the front a woman stood before the people.

"Let us praise the Lord with joyful voices," she said.

For the next ten minutes, voices in the church blended in happy song. Hands clapped and feet stomped. It was a joyful gathering.

But then a man got up in front and started yelling. "You are all sinners!" he screamed. "The Lord is angry at you all!"

On and on the man went, his voice hurting my ears. Surely the good Lord did not intend that people hear only about "the evil ways of living." I was grateful when the people began to sing again.

"Did you like the church service?" Mrs. Martin asked when I got home.

I nodded, remembering the happy music and joyful songs. "But I like it when we pray together each morning," I added.

Yes, every morning Mr. Martin read the words from the Bible, just like Master Carver used to do. Sometimes he let me read, too. We even made up our own prayers.

To please the Martins, I went back to church the next Sunday. As I was leaving, a strange woman grabbed my arm.

"You come here by yourself, boy?" The thin dark woman brushed a wisp of grey hair from her forehead making a bracelet jingle on her wrist. "I seen you last week and this week, too. It's a good strong soul that will bring hisself to church on his own at your age."

With that, the woman turned and hurried off. People nodded at her and smiled. "Hello, Aunt Mariah," some of them greeted her. "How are you feeling today?"

After the next church service, I waited where I knew Aunt Mariah would pass by. She stopped and invited me to her home.

A cleaner place I had never seen. It was only one room, but it sat bright and spotless as it welcomed in the afternoon sun. Colorful rag rugs dotted the floor. Rich smells of spices hung in the air. In the corner stood a giant washtub and board.

"I takes in washings," Aunt Mariah announced proudly. "Cleanliness is next to godliness. It's a right respectable trade."

After that first visit, I returned often to Aunt Mariah's home. On my third visit I met Uncle Andy. Aunt Mariah had spoken little of her husband. "A good man," she said of him, "but taken to drink, the devil's sickness."

"Devil's sickness." I had heard others speak of the wicked desire for liquor and ale. Uncle Andy's heavy drinking kept him from steady work. So it fell to Aunt Mariah to take in washing to survive.

Despite the devil's sickness, Uncle Andy knew well the Lord's words. But he did not obey God's way. Often the three of us sat in the yard, sharing stories from the Bible.

One night after supper, John and Lucy Martin seemed very quiet. I knew something was wrong—very wrong.

"Have—have I done something bad?" I asked, looking up from the hearth. "Are you angry with me?"

John puffed on his pipe, while Lucy sat darning a shawl.

"No," John answered. "We are anything but angry. We've enjoyed having you with us."

"You have been a gift from God," Lucy Martin added, in a tone edged with sadness.

"But we are going to be moving west," her husband said, looking at his pipe. "You will have to find a new home."

How happy I had been with the Martins. Never did

I think about our life together ending. I could not stop the tears that clouded my eyes. A new home. Where would I go?

"You'll come live with us," Aunt Mariah declared the next day. "I'll be grateful for the help. But you'll not stop your schoolin', that is one thing certain."

I hugged Aunt Mariah tightly. The Lord was surely watching over me.

Eagerly I returned to the classroom when school opened again. Soon I could read and figure sums better than anyone in the school. Sometimes I even caught the schoolmaster making mistakes, an act that only earned me angry frowns. Folks I worked for around Neosho said I should go after more schooling.

"Kansas is bursting with good schools," one storekeeper told me. "Go to Fort Scott. That's a lively town with a fine school."

I thought a long time about leaving. Aunt Mariah and Uncle Andy would be sad, but finally I knew the time had come.

"We'll miss you, George," Aunt Mariah told me. "Just don't you forget us. Here, take this with you."

In her hands Aunt Mariah clutched a leather book. It was a Bible.

"Thank you, ma'am," I answered. "I will use it every day and think of you."

I packed my few things in a small bundle and headed out of Neosho. A morning wind whipped the Missouri dust into my face. I had only walked for an hour, when a mule team pulling an old wagon came bumping along behind me.

"Where you headed, boy?" the driver shouted down.

"Fort Scott, Kansas," I yelled up. "I'll be glad to

share the reins with you. It would give you some sleepin' time."

The driver smiled. "A good trade. Jump up here. I could use some rest." He took off his straw hat to wipe the sweat from his forehead.

"Happy to," I agreed, scrambling up and taking the reins. The driver crawled into the back of the wagon. Within minutes, I could hear his deep snores.

As I snapped the reins, I looked on down the long road. The flat fields stretched as far as I could see. Somewhere in the distance lay Fort Scott, Kansas.

But beyond that place my path was unclear. I prayed the good Lord would give me direction.

Journey to Nowhere

"Whoa—whoa, boy!"

As the driver of the mule wagon slowed his team, I jumped down. "Thanks for the ride!" I hollered. Slowly I looked around at Fort Scott.

It was a busy place, that much was easy to tell. A stagecoach and buggies rolled along the dusty streets. Clusters of cattlemen, farmers, and ranchers stood talking on every corner. Ladies visited outside store windows, sharing talk about new dresses and hats. I chuckled, watching a lone black dog dash from one rolling carriage to another, nipping at the wooden wheels. No one seemed interested in the poor mongrel's fate. I hoped I would not receive the same treatment.

Fortunately I did not. The first day after my arrival I found a job. It was helping at The Wilder House, the fanciest hotel in town. My work was to do the laundry daily and then stack it neatly.

The linen was kept in a huge room. The pale towels

were stacked in four giant piles, the white linens in six. On my first day at work I looked at a mirror on the wall. There I stood, like a black crow in a cotton field. The sight made me laugh.

The hotel manager let me sleep on the back porch. By heating up the stove each morning and washing dishes, I earned my meals.

One morning I stopped before the golden trimmed mirror in the lobby of The Wilder House. It was far bigger than the one in the linen room. As I looked at myself, I shook my head in disgust. Thirteen I was, yet I looked like a boy often. How I longed to grow taller. Then I would not have to stand on a stool to reach the washtubs as I worked. Surely it was a strain for the Lord to see all of us small folk. Still, it was said, "His eye is on the sparrow." So I knew He was watching me.

Carefully I arranged my daily work hours so I could enroll at the high school. The school was a sturdy brick building on the town square. I soon discovered the schoolmistress was a mite friendlier than my schoolmaster had been in Neosho, Missouri.

"You spell right well, George," she told me after my first week. "But you must learn to write the words clearly, too."

My favorite class was nature study. Few of the other students could make the bird calls as I could. We read about plants and soil—the things I loved most. I spent hours drawing pictures of beautiful flowers and leaves.

Going to school in Fort Scott was a special joy. But there were days when I missed Frau and Master Carver, the Martins, Aunt Mariah and Uncle Andy.

As I sat in my geography class one afternoon, my

mind wandered back to my early years. I took a piece
of paper and began drawing. Suddenly my thoughts
were interrupted by the instructor's voice.

"George Washington Carver, what are you doing?"

I gulped deeply, surprised at being caught. "I've just
been drawing." A tingling feeling swept through my
whole body to my face.

"Please bring me your artwork."

Slowly I trudged forward, carrying the piece of paper. She took it from me and examined it closely.

"Where are these hills?" she asked.

"They are in the Ozarks," I answered, my voice unable to hide my fear. "They're the foothills."

"Is this where you lived?"

I nodded.

"Well, I want you to stop in after school tonight. I
want to show your picture to Miss Long. She might
take you into her drawing class."

Miss Long's Drawing Class? Only a few students
were allowed to work with Miss Long. As I returned
to my seat, I could hardly wait for school to end. But
like always when I wished time to fly by, it slowed to a
crawl.

Finally the day was over. I hurried back to my geography classroom. Miss Long was standing by the
doorway. She was holding my picture.

"This is fine work, George," she said. "You show
artistic talent. Beginning next week you will come to
my drawing class."

"Hal-le-lujah!" I blurted out, forgetting I was in the
classroom. Miss Long just shook her head, but I thought
I saw her grin a mite as she walked away.

Weeks drifted into months. My whole life centered

around school. I did my chores at The Wilder House, but every extra minute I spent at school.

Miss Long gave me a box of water colors for Christmas. I could hardly control my joy. "Double Hallelujah!" I shouted.

The hot weather and summer holidays brought the desire to travel, to see more of the world. When a traveler visited The Wilder House looking for railroad workers, I signed up.

My new job was quite an adventure. Most of the time I spent helping the cook. The railroad men ate with giant appetites. Never did I meet so many different kinds of people.

Despite the excitement of the new job, I had no intention of giving up my schooling. Soon I returned to the classroom. In 1885, when I was twenty-one years old, I graduated from high school.

My high school work completed, there was but one place I wanted to go. Eagerly I boarded a train and headed back to the Ozark Mountains to see Master Carver and his good wife.

I had not even reached the cabin when I saw Frau Carver come running off the porch. "Oh, George," she cried, hugging me tight. "All grown up you are."

The Master's handshake felt strong and firm. But the warmth of his hug felt even better.

"So you are high school educated," he said, smiling. "Well, you are surely welcome to come back with us."

I nodded gratefully and smiled, "Thank you, Master Carver, but I'm going on to college."

Frau Carver looked surprised. "But I didn't know Negroes could go to college."

Quickly I pulled a letter from my back pocket. "I am going to Highland University in Kansas. They have awarded me a scholarship for my grades in high school. I must report there September 13."

The news pleased Master and Frau Carver. Their eyes widened as they read the letter.

"You have made us proud," the Master declared. "I am happy you carry the name Carver."

The days slipped by quickly. No sooner had I again come to know the woods and hills when it was time to leave. Once more I left the Carvers standing on the cabin porch. This time I turned and waved back happily.

Highland University was a small school. When I arrived at the main office, I was told to report to the President.

Entering the president's big office, I gazed around in amazement. Books lined every wall to the ceiling! Behind a wide desk sat a bald man with his glasses perched on a rather stout nose. When he saw me, his eyes widened and his mouth dropped open.

"I am George Washington Carver," I said. The

words tumbled out in a strong whisper. I held my sweating hands behind my back, not wanting the man to notice I was trembling.

Slowly the president removed his glasses and rubbed his eyes. He looked tired. "Young man, I'm afraid there has been a mistake," he said softly. "We cannot enroll you here at Highland."

"But I have your letter of acceptance!" I exclaimed. "You told me to come today and I am here."

The man shook his head. "You failed to inform us you were colored. We do not take colored students here at Highland."

My thoughts were jumbled. Desperately I searched for words. "I spent all my money to come here. I have nothing left. I want to study here, to learn. I answered all the questions on the application."

Replacing his glasses on his nose, the man again turned his attention to the papers on his desk. "Mister Carver, this conversation is ended. There is no use talking further."

"It isn't fair," I argued, my voice rising. "I cannot come to study here because my skin is black?"

"I believe you understand," the man answered, not looking up. "Now if you don't mind, I have work to do."

My head felt dizzy. Somehow I stumbled outside. Nowhere. That is where I was. My money was gone and I had nowhere to go.

For the first time in my life I felt completely alone. The Lord, the good and merciful Lord I had always trusted, seemed to have cast me aside.

"Why?" I asked, tears filling my eyes. "What have I done to offend Thee?"

Caught in a Blizzard

For hours I wandered alone around the university town. Along the streets students stood happily chatting. How I longed to share their talk. It looked like such a wonderful life.

But it was not to be my life. My future lay along a different path. Thankfully, it was time for the field harvests. Walking to a peaceful-looking farm not far from town, I hired on as an extra worker.

"You can stay as long as you want," the farm owner told me. "If you're needing a place to sleep, the hay in the loft is freshly mowed."

Once again a mound of hay became my bed. That night, as I stared up at the star-filled sky, I wondered if my life would ever change. It mattered little that I had finished high school. I was back to where I began—sleeping on hay.

"Yes," I murmured to myself, "I will work and save my money. Surely there is some college which will take colored people. I have to read more, to study and learn."

The other farmhands were friendly and kind. Most were surprised when they learned I had completed high school. Like the Carvers, they were astonished at my hopes of going to college.

"Ain't never heard of such a thing!" one man laughed. "A blackie in college? Yep, that's a new one all right!"

Carefully I saved my money. As more and more folks talked about "homesteading," a new urge began to grow inside me. Homesteaders were people who settled on western land, planted crops, and cared for livestock. It sounded like a good life, clean and honest.

In the year 1886, news reached us that the government was giving away free land in West Kansas. All a person had to do was file a claim and agree to live on that land. I had never owned any land. It was too exciting an adventure to let slip by. So it was that at twenty-two, I joined a wagon train west, settled in Ness County, Kansas, and filed a claim on 160 acres.

With winter approaching, I began building a cabin. It was a small structure—a building some might call a hut. But inside its four walls were two strong chairs, a bed, and a stove to cook food and keep out the fierce wintry winds.

Finding I had spent all my money to build my house, I decided to seek work at a nearby farm. A rancher to the south hired me on to keep his stable clean and his livestock fed.

When winter months drifted into spring, my 160 acres took on new joy and beauty. The soil was not rich enough for crops, but suitable for grazing. Since I had no livestock, that offered me little reward.

Still, the land was mine, all mine. Wild flowers blossomed everywhere, dotting the rolling landscape with bright colors. Berries and herbs flourished, providing me with food and nourishment. Each day I ventured into the open countryside with my pencils and paints. The hours slipped swiftly by as I drew and painted. By dusk I returned to my home with picture upon picture of the scenes of my special world. Each changing season brought new beauty to the Kansas prairie.

One autumn morning I set out shortly after sunrise. There was a crispness to the air, signaling the winter ahead. Soon I knew I had to decide whether to hire out for the months ahead or remain in my home. I had made many friends among the area farmers during my three years on the prairie. Work would be easy to find.

"Tomorrow is for decisions," I told myself. "Today is for painting."

A prairie dog dashed for his hole as I approached. His tiny eyes blazed in the cave he called his home. He and his neighbors yelped loudly at me.

Overhead a pair of eagles played their games in the sky. How gracefully they soared upward, then swooped suddenly to catch a scurrying gopher on the ground below.

Carefully I set my paints upon a large rock. Another stone nearby provided me a seat while I worked. Minutes slipped into hours as I sketched the bloom of an autumn primrose that lay nestled in a patch of blue grama grass.

Suddenly I felt a bitter chill. Tiny needles seemed to pierce my skin. A sandstorm? No, the specks were not sand. They were snowflakes, sharp and cold. Quickly I gathered my things and headed back to my cabin.

The snowflakes multiplied. I had heard stories about

the dreaded Kansas blizzards, and I had no desire to become caught in one. My quick steps became a steady run.

Sharp winds ripped across the flat prairie, tossing bushes into the air. The sky was a dismal rolling sea of grey mist.

A strong breeze caught the canvas I was carrying and snapped it away. I turned, trying to grab it, but it tumbled wildly away in the icy flakes. I stumbled forward on the ground. A burning pain shot through my right leg. I lay back on the hard soil. Maybe after a little rest the pain would go away.

But after several minutes, I knew I could not linger. The snow was falling thick and heavy. It stuck to my hair and clothes. Melting flakes ran into my eyes. Snow formed small mounds and hills as the winds raked it across the plains. I had to get home, back to my cabin. Slowly lifting myself up, I hobbled forward.

It was at least an hour before my cabin came into view. My skin felt burned from the mean winds. My leg throbbed, probably from a torn muscle or bad bruise.

"Thank you for getting me home safely, dear Lord," I stopped, the words choking in my throat. I had prayed little since being turned away from the university. In my years here on the prairie, I had felt a distance between the Lord and myself. In some way that I did not know, I thought I had offended Him. He had cast me aside, allowing me to suffer bitter rejection.

Another strong wind pushed me toward the cabin. I stumbled wearily to the doorway. The snow was already starting to bank against one side of the building.

Once inside, I built a giant fire in the stove. Thank-

fully, my food and wood supply were both well stocked.
Soon I collapsed on my cot, grateful for the sleep that
came swiftly.

Hours later, I awakened with a sense of unknown
fear. My cabin looked so small and closed in. The reason became clear at once. The ceiling sagged sadly
under the weight of heavy snow. Would it break, dumping its load of snow on me? The thought of being
crushed and smothered by the ice numbed me.

Slowly moving to the doorway, I tried to push it
open. It slid back only an inch, enough to reveal a thick
five-foot drift. I could not get outside to knock the snow
off the roof.

A log snapped in the stove. I hurried to again build
up the fire. I hoped the heat would help melt the snow.
A wind shook the cabin, leaving eerie whistling echoes
as it passed.

Carefully I planned how to save food. I was certain the supply would last six or seven days.

But what if the snow remained longer than that? What then? I shivered, not from the cold of the wind, but from a coldness within my soul. Even in my cabin, I was lost in this blizzard. Who would have reason to come here? No one. I was alone, all alone. No one cared what happened to me.

The hours passed slowly. I slept, trying to avoid activity which would build hunger. The woodpile grew smaller.

One night as I slept, a clear dream entered my mind. I saw a white mound upon a sparkling landscape. Suddenly I sat up, rubbing my eyes. The picture was still clear to me. It was my cabin buried under the snow. A frozen tomb. An unknown grave.

Alone. How I longed for the sound of a voice, the sight of a smile, the touch of a hand. Alone. Had any one ever felt so alone?

And then another picture formed in my mind. A man, a lone figure stumbling into a desert. For forty days and forty nights He wandered. The Lord—a sad and lonely Lord.

Perhaps, just perhaps, He had His own plan for my life. Was the rejection at the university part of it? Had He brought me here to this desert? Perhaps I had not offended Him at all.

Slowly the deep tortured feeling of loneliness slipped away. No longer did I feel alone. A new presence was with me in the cabin. Someone did care about me. The Lord knew where I was. He had a plan for me.

"Show me the way," I begged, slipping to my knees beside the bed. "Give me the directions You have for my life."

After six days of cold and gloom, the morning brought a bright warm sun. Heat. Blazing heat.

Tiny drops soon turned to narrow streams as the snow melted under the sun's burning rays.

By late afternoon I pushed the heavy door open. Across the white crust I watched the sun setting.

Free. Once more I was free.

And within me I felt a strong desire to once again be with people. I wanted to help and serve them. This was *His* plan; I was sure of it. I would sell my land and change my life.

Never again would I be alone. Whatever the future held, I knew the Lord would be with me.

Magic Hands

Slowly the buggy bumped and rumbled along the dusty Iowa road. A tired wooden sign appeared nailed to a fence post.

"Indianola," the sign read. I grinned, giving the reins a hearty snap. A strong summer breeze stirred through the rows of rich Iowa corn.

"I'll be leaving you here," I told the red-bearded man next to me. "I'm much obliged to you for sharing your buggy."

My friend nodded, taking the reins. "So there's a college in this town, is there? I knew there was plenty of feed and hardware stores. But I ain't never heard of a college here."

"Simpson College is its name," I answered. "A man named Bishop Mathew Simpson started it with all the money and land he owned." I picked up my small package of belongings.

"And they take coloreds?" His raised thick eyebrows reflected his surprise.

I felt a wide smile cross my face. "They sure do. Bishop Simpson was a right good friend of President

Abraham Lincoln. They both looked out for us colored folks."

As the buggy lurched slowly through Indianola, I
jumped off. Inside my pants pocket, I felt for the few
coins I had left. The trip from Kansas had eaten away
at the ten dollars I had gotten for my cabin and land.
But the letter from Simpson College had promised a
room to any student needing one. Hopefully, I could
find some work to pay for food, some clothes, and . . .

"You're an awful big black man!"

A strange voice interrupted my thoughts. Looking
down, I saw a young girl, her blonde hair neatly piled
into a bun on top of her head. She licked a large red
lollipop which had already coated her chin and lips into
a deep sticky pink.

"Yes, little girl, that's what I am." I smiled and bent
down. But before I could say more, a tall woman with
a pinched-looking mouth rushed over. She grabbed
the little girl's hand and pulled her away.

Rising once more, I rubbed my chin. It was clear
enough that no matter where I traveled, folks were a
mite suspicious of this black skin I wore.

The welcome at Simpson College was friendly indeed. Smiles and nods greeted me from every direction. It seemed that I was the only black student regis-
tering. At twenty-six, I was older than most of the others starting college. I could not keep my hand steady
as I filled out my registration card. This was a new
chapter in my life—a new beginning. Beside the tiny
box on the card marked major, I wrote one word—
"art." Yes, I was eager to continue drawing and painting. Maybe, with hard work and study, I could some-
day become a great artist or teacher. I could not think

of a better way to share the beauty of God's world
with others.

The college furnished every student with a small
room. Each contained a bed, chair, and little desk. With
the thirteen cents I had left, I bought a large bag of
cornmeal and a package of suet. The food would feed
me for a week. Then I hoped to find work and earn
some coins.

Jobs were plentiful around the college. Few of the
white students could mend and sew or wash and press
clothes. How often in my prayers I thanked Frau Carver
for her teaching. My art teacher, Miss Budd, helped
find me an empty woodshed on the campus. It served
nicely as a headquarters for my "clothes fix-it shop."

"Hope you got time for patching up a pair of my
pants, George," one classmate greeted me. "My back-
side is beginning to feel those winter breezes."

"Got any small white buttons?" another friend asked. "I'm missing three off this shirt."

Some nights the woodshed got right crowded. Jokes were exchanged and stories told. Every now and then we even did some studying.

College days passed quickly. Miss Budd displayed many of my paintings on different walls across the small campus. But she was not satisfied with me working only on canvas.

"Your fingers are long and thin," she told me one afternoon. "Have you ever played a piano?"

I nodded, remembering a few times when Mrs. Mueller had let me touch her fine instrument after working in the garden. "But I've never taken lessons," I added hastily.

Miss Budd squeezed a few final drops of water from a paintbrush. "Then it's time you did!" she declared.

The next week piano lessons joined my college studies. Before long I became a member of the college chorus, too. I loved the songs that praised the Lord. How fast the hours slipped by with activity. Like the words from Job, "My days were swifter than a weaver's shuttle."

Early one morning I hurried from my art class to my nature lab. We were studying plant stems, and I was assigned to make a presentation. Under my arm, I held a long canvas covered by a piece of worn calico cloth.

"You got your speech under there, George?" a classmate teased as I entered the room.

"Could be," I answered.

I could hardly wait to begin. Once the teacher introduced me, I pulled off the cloth. My classmates gasped.

"Here is a drawing which shows the major kinds of

plant stems," I explained. "Sunlight, water, good soil—all contribute to the growth of the healthy stem . . ."

My talk went on for almost half an hour. When it was over, my classmates applauded. The instructor approached me with an unusual request.

"I'd like to keep your chart, Mr. Carver," he said. "Future classes would profit from your drawings. I have never seen such perfect likenesses. They almost seem to live."

The words were kind, and the applause echoed in my ears as I left the lab that day. But the wise words of Proverbs 16:18 softened the applause: "Pride goeth before destruction, and a haughty spirit before a fall."

I began spending more and more time in the lab. What exciting secrets lay within blossoms and leaves! It was one thing to paint the creations of God, but another still to help them grow. I came to truly enjoy working with His world of nature.

"We have given you all we can here at Simpson," my biology instructor told me one day. "Find a school where you can continue your studies. Like these plants, you must grow also."

Carefully I wrestled with the decision. It could not be made lightly. I was twenty-seven years old. I knew all doors were not open to those of my race. Whether it be more school or work, I knew my decision had to be made with care, but not alone.

"Lord, help me," I prayed.

The decision did not come easily. After much prayer, I felt the Lord was directing me to seek more education. In the fall of 1891, I enrolled at Iowa State College in Ames. The faculty and modern laboratories at Iowa State were considered among the best in the country.

Still, there was one major problem. No Negro students were allowed to live in the dormitory.

As I explained this problem to Mr. Wilson, one of the college directors, his face reddened.

"That's a ridiculous rule!" he exclaimed, pounding his desk with a fist. "I'll work to get it changed. In the meantime, you may sleep in my college office. We want you as a student here!"

I nodded, grateful for the gentleman's help. The next day we moved a mattress into his office on the campus. It was quite a scene.

"This is like carrying a giant jellyfish!" Mr. Wilson shouted, juggling his end of the soft padding.

"It will be the softest bed I've ever slept upon," I added.

It took two hours to finish the job. Twice the mattress got stuck in the doorway. It was not the only thing that got stuck. Mr. Wilson found himself pushed against the wall. I did not escape either. As we dropped the mattress, it flopped on top of me. I almost smothered under the goose feathers.

Iowa State was a fine school. I met each day eagerly, delighted to get to my classes. My cot was always surrounded by books and papers. Often I visited my friends in the dormitories for study sessions.

Late one night, I left a friend's room after studying. The dormitory hallway was long and dark. Suddenly, I heard loud groaning. I stopped, a bit frightened. The sounds were coming from down the hall. Slowly, I tiptoed forward.

As the groans grew louder, the sounds seemed more agonizing. I stopped in front of a closed door from where the moans seemed to be coming. I rapped lightly.

There was no answer. Again I knocked.

This time the door slid open. A dim light beside the bed revealed a large huddled figure. It was a boy of about twenty, his face muscles twisted in pain.

"Can I help you?" I whispered, stepping nearer to the bed. "Is there anything you need?"

For a moment the boy forced himself to stop moaning. "It's my legs—my whole body. It hurts all over. I think I've bruised every muscle. I just can't stand the pain."

"What happened to you? Where did you get hurt?"

"It was at football practice—" Before he could finish, the moans started again. I slipped to the edge of the bed beside him.

"Roll over," I ordered. "Lie as flat on your stomach as you can."

The boy obeyed, still groaning. Slowly and carefully I began rubbing the backs of his legs. From the ankles to the thighs my hands pressed deeply. The muscles were hard and stiff. His skin was hot. Back and forth I rubbed, over and over.

In a few moments the boy stopped moaning. Steady breathing replaced the painful moans. Soon the husky boy was asleep.

Silently I stood up and slipped out the door. I was grateful to rest my own body that night, tired as it was from the work it had done.

As I hurried to my first class the next morning, a new friend caught up to me and grabbed my arm.

"Hey, you've got magic in those hands of yours," he laughed. "I don't know how you did it, but I feel great this morning. No pain at all."

"Good," I exclaimed. "I'm glad I could help."

"Just keep those hands in good shape," the boy said, turning to go. "They've really got magic in them!"

I watched the boy run off, then gazed down at my hands. "Magic hands indeed!" I laughed. "Now if *I* only knew what to do with them!"

Surprise Meeting

I stood ankle deep in mud. I had come to this swampland which belonged to the college to gather samples of plants. Stooping to observe a patch of leaves more closely, I suddenly heard a strange slurping sound. My body tensed. What could be out in this lonely swamp with me?

Again I heard the sounds—loud sucking sounds. Footsteps! That's what they were. But the heavy, thick mud gave an eerie echo to the movement of feet. The footsteps came more closely together, moving more rapidly, too rapidly through the mud. Whoever this intruder was knew little about the muddy 'suckholes' scattered throughout this dangerous swampland. Some of the holes were bottomless, eager to become deep graves for innocent, unsuspecting victims.

A spot of color appeared behind a cluster of tall grasses. The spot was yellow and red, a plaid that contrasted sharply with the drabness of the swamp. I tucked my specimen basket under one arm and cupped my free hand above my eyes to block out the sun.

My heartbeat quickened. I saw the figure clearly now, beyond the row of grasses. It was a boy who looked about ten. He sprang like a red plaid frog, leaping from one mudhole to another. He seemed to be playing a game. It was clear he did not know that one of the mudholes might become a deathtrap and pull him in. The game could be fatal.

"Hey!" I yelled. "Watch where you're stepping!"

For just a brief moment the boy stopped. Then, after a short pause, he jumped to another mud pocket.

"Stop right there!" I ordered. "Don't jump any more. Don't make a move."

This time the boy saw me. He stood waiting as I cautiously moved toward him.

"You can't go running and jumping through here," I said. "Do you know you could fall and be smothered in this mud?"

The boy's eyes widened. Such a thought had obviously never occurred to him. "But-but you're here," he stammered. "Why are you here?"

It was a fair question. "I am a student at the college. Some of us come here to study the plants and mud soil. This is a specimen basket where I have put samples of the grass and dirt."

A confused look still crossed the boy's face. "But I wasn't hurting anything."

Moving behind the boy, I bent down. "Look at this. A muskrat worked very hard to build his home here. You just knocked down one whole wall. Your home is in town. Muskrats are supposed to live in this swamp. The Lord provides the right homes for His creatures."

Carefully the boy looked at the crushed leaves and grasses in the mud. "I stepped on his home?"

I nodded, noticing the boy's eyes filling with tears. He was truly sorry for what he had done.

"What is your name?" I asked.

The boy hesitated a minute. "Henry. Henry Wallace. My father teaches at the college. But I hope you won't tell him what I did."

"Professor Wallace?" I exclaimed. "Why, he's one of my teachers. He teaches dairy science."

The boy nodded. "Sometimes my father lets me visit the dairy station and watch the cows being milked. What's your name?"

"George Washington Carver," I replied. "It's alot safer visiting the dairy station than running around out here. It's cleaner too."

For the first time, the boy smiled. He wiped some of the thick mud from his legs. "If I stay with you, will you show me how you find specimens? And will you tell me what you do with the grass and mud?"

"That sounds like a worthy agreement," I answered. "Maybe you will show me around the dairy station and tell me what you know about it."

Young Henry Wallace extended his mud-speckled hand. "That's fair enough. I hope we can be good friends."

In the months that followed, we became just that. Henry was an eager, interested companion. He never seemed to run out of questions.

"Why do some plants fold up their leaves at night? What makes some ears of corn big and others little?"

The questions came quickly. Often I had to do extra reading and asking in class to provide Henry with answers.

There were other questions too—on tests, in discussions, with lab equipment. Surely there was no busier place than Iowa State College. Each night I collapsed on my cot, exhausted from the day's activities. But I was happy, too. It was wonderful being able to study and learn, to explore secrets of the Lord's wonderful world.

Like all the other male students, I was required to take the Military Tactics course at the college. Some days we marched and did exercises. On other days we read about battles and methods of fighting. I found little pleasure in the course. There was more excitement in the lab, discovering God's wonders of life and living creatures.

"If ever I must kill," I prayed to the Lord nightly, "let it be the evil temptations within me."

In the spring of 1894, when I was thirty I received my bachelor's degree from Iowa State College. My military training earned me a captain's commission in the National Guard.

"Congratulations!" Professor Wilson told me. "You're the first Negro to graduate from this school and, I think, the first to become a captain in the National Guard. You should be very proud, George."

"Thank you," I answered, a trace of worry in my voice. I felt some pride in my accomplishments, but I had no job and no place to go. My future was uncertain.

One evening, as I was packing my suitcase for an unknown destination, Professor Wilson pounded on my door. Before I could open it, he barged in.

"Don't pack those bags too quickly," Professor Wilson said. "You're not going anywhere."

My open mouth and confused look revealed complete surprise. "Not going?" I blurted out. What could the professor mean?

"You've been hired here at the college," my friend continued. "You'll teach botany and be in charge of the greenhouses. Now come with me. My good wife is preparing a feast in your honor. It's time to celebrate!"

I had no time to grab a cap or sweater as Professor Wilson pulled me quickly out the door. My heart pounded with excitement as we walked. The stars sparkled in the dark sky like a million fireflies against black graphite.

"Your job here should not come as a surprise," Professor Wilson said as we walked swiftly across the campus. "Your grades have been outstanding. Who would be better able to care for the greenhouse and teach botany?"

A teacher at Iowa State College. Me! It did not seem possible. Surely this time the Lord had outdone Himself!

But in my joy, I could not conceal some concern. It was one thing to be a student, quite another to be a teacher. Could I do such a job? Did I know enough?

"Lord, do not stray far," I murmured, knowing He had promised in Matthew 28:20, "Lo, I am with you alway."

"I will be needing You now more than ever."

A Plea for Help

A pair of hands covered my eyes as I knelt beside a large potted fern plant. I had heard no one enter the greenhouse.

"Guess who it is?" a voice squealed.

"Christopher Columbus," I answered. "And if it's not Chris, it must be Henry Wallace."

Henry laughed and knelt beside me. His laughter was replaced by a worried frown as he looked at the fern.

"What are all those ugly spots?" the twelve-year-old boy asked. "Those white and brown circles?"

"They're called scales. The white ones are young insects that move from plant to plant on the fern leaves. The others are older and stay where they are. As they grow they eat the fern leaves which eventually kills the plant."

Henry looked alarmed, moving closer. "Can you stop them?" he asked.

"I hope so," I replied, pointing to a test tube on a nearby table. "That solution I've mixed has to be wiped on the leaves every four hours. It should kill the scales."

"Does that mean you'll have to stay up all night?" Henry asked.

I nodded. "There's no other way."

Henry smiled. "My father said he used to stay up all night with me when I cried and everything. I guess these plants are like your children."

I chuckled and rested a hand on my friend's shoulder. So these plants were my children, were they? The thought had more than a thimble full of truth to it. Yes, I did watch over God's plants, providing them with food and nourishment to keep them healthy. I cared for the sick ones, too.

A line from Psalm 144 stirred in my mind, "That our sons may be as plants grown up in their youth." I smiled broadly—surely a plant was among the finest of the Lord's creations and deserved the best care man could provide.

"Come on, Henry, I believe we have a rose to inspect."

Eagerly the young boy followed. He shared the thrills and adventure of the greenhouse with me. It was a special place to us—each day offering new paths to discovery.

Henry found much excitement in grafting. Carefully we grafted a branch from a red rose bush to a yellow rose bush. This was done by slitting the bark of one and splicing in a tiny cutting of the other. The lad was full of questions.

"Why are we grafting this rose?"

"Grafting can speed up growing times," I answered. "Sometimes a plant is not strong enough to grow all on its own in a particular climate. But if its stem is grafted

into the stem of a more hardy plant, it will live."

My days as a college professor at Iowa State College were no longer frightening. Teaching proved joyful and I continued my own studies. In the spring of 1896, I received my master's degree in agriculture. I enjoyed writing articles about my plant discoveries for magazines and journals.

"You have become famous," Professor Wilson told me one night after dinner. He raised his feet and rested them on top of his desk. "Your work with plants and plant diseases is well known. Every meeting I attend I hear people talking about George Washington Carver at Iowa State."

The words were pleasing to me. "But for every answer I find, there are two more questions," I said.

Professor Wilson smiled. "That is the sign of a true scientist. You know, George, there is one story about you I do find hard to believe. Someone told me you can grow corn on a bare wood floor."

My laughter rocked the room as I plopped back in my chair. That was the best joke I had ever heard.

"Just keep growing your corn here with us," kind Professor Wilson said. "We want you to stay with us a long time."

But a strange letter arrived a few weeks later that changed my life. Surprised, I held the letter saying, "Who, what? Mail seldom comes to me." Although I shared my plant research often by writing newspaper and magazine articles, I was truly no letter writer.

The crumpled and battered envelope bearing my name looked like it had come a great distance. But the handwriting inside was clear to the eye. I glanced at the signature on the bottom, "Dr. Booker T. Washington, President, Tuskegee Institute, Alabama."

The names of Dr. Washington and his Tuskegee school were not unknown to me. Fifteen years ago he had opened his institute designed to train Negro teachers and students.

Slowly I began to read the letter:

Tuskegee Institute seeks to provide education—a means for survival to those who attend. Our students are poor, often starving. They travel miles of torn roads, across years of poverty. We teach them to read and write, but words cannot fill stomachs. They need to learn how to plant and harvest crops.

For a moment I stopped reading. Years drifted away as I recalled the hungry and lean faces of the boys and girls at the Neosho School in Missouri. They, too, had little and fought each day to stay alive. But the picture Dr. Washington painted with words was one of thousands of poor, starving young people. It was a sad picture.

In his letter Dr. Washington shared the history of Tuskegee—fulfillment of his hopes and dreams. He wanted me to leave Iowa State and come to teach at Tuskegee Institute. Finally, I reached the last part of the letter:

I cannot offer you money, position, or fame. The first two you have. The last, from the place you now occupy, you will no doubt achieve. These things I now ask you to give up. I offer you in their place work—hard, hard work and the challenge of bringing people from degradation, poverty, and waste to full manhood.

Slowly I slipped the letter inside the crumpled envelope. I left the greenhouse and walked across the campus. Students and friends greeted me, but I barely noticed. My mind was far away—deep in the South. What should I do? What was the Lord's plan for me?

For hours I walked. So many memories floated back. I remembered one more clearly than any other—how I was refused and turned away at Highland University. Now Tuskegee was accepting Negro students. What would be their experience upon arrival? Would they find a shortage of teachers and courses?

The sun was setting in the west as I returned to my small room. The Lord had outdone Himself, splashing the sky with streaks of bright orange and purple that evening.

Sitting down at the wooden desk near my bed, I took a piece of paper and a pen. "I will come," I wrote. The words looked simple and plain. There seemed no need to say anything more.

The next weeks were not easy ones as I prepared to leave. Everyone at the college treated me kindly, sadly accepting my decision.

Professor Wilson tapped his horse lightly with the whip as he drove me to the train station. As we got out of his buggy, he took a large package from under the seat. "This is for you," he said, "from your friends here."

My fingers trembled as they untied the string around the package. When I saw what it was, my eyes widened in surprise. A microscope!

"It's so you won't forget us in your new lab at Tuskegee," Professor Wilson said.

I nodded, firmly squeezing Professor Wilson's hand. "You did not need to give me this. I would never forget anyone here in Iowa. If only . . ."

The locomotive hissed in the background. "All a-b-o-a-r-d!" the conductor called.

Quickly I boarded the train, cradling my microscope carefully. The thread of cars pulled away from the station.

My stomach churned. How I would miss my lab, the greenhouse, and my students. But then these things would be waiting in Alabama. "I am not losing anything," I thought. "I am only changing my location."

Little did I know the surprises that lay ahead.

Strange Treasure

Clickety-clack . . . clickety-clack . . .

The heavy steel wheels of the train repeated their song over and over on the track. I gazed out of my window in the passenger car and watched the dark Iowa soil fade quickly as we rolled southward.

The October air was unusually hot and sticky. I dabbed my forehead with a handkerchief.

When the train reached St. Louis, Missouri, a sad-faced conductor made his way to my seat.

"Uh—sir," he began, his blue eyes looking downward. "You'll have to—ah—move back to the next car." Clumsily the man pulled at a button on his vest. Never once did he look at me directly.

I arose, carefully holding on to my new microscope with one hand and my small clothes bag with the other. I moved to a car crowded with members of my own race. Yes, the trains in the South still had their "Jim-Crow Cars" to keep the blacks from the whites. We had won our freedom in 1863 with Lincoln's help, but

our place was still not beside the white man. In my
clothes bag, I carried three certificates of education—
a high school diploma and two college degrees. In the
good year of 1896, they mattered little as we rumbled
along in the Southland.

Eagerly I awaited my meeting with President Booker
T. Washington. But he was not waiting at the Alabama
station. Instead, a thin lad of about twenty stood beside a fine buggy. A pair of handsome horses stood
before it.

"Are you Master Carver from Iowa?" the young
man asked.

"Master." It was strange to have anyone call me
"Master." It had seemed a proper label for old farmer
Carver. But now . . . "Mister Carver suits me better," I
answered gently, juggling my microscope into the same
arm that held my traveling bag. I extended my free hand
for shaking.

My new friend looked surprised and pleased. He

accepted my hand in a firm shake, then reached out for
my clothes bag. "President Washington is waiting for
us," he said, leading me to the buggy. "The school is
about three miles from here.

Alabama and Iowa. Two different worlds. I gazed
over the bright reddish colored banks of clay as we
rode and recalled the deep, black soil in Iowa. The
buggy squeaked and moaned beneath our weight as it
bumped in and out of the cracks in the dirt road. I
brushed the dust off my jacket as the carriage finally
stopped before a building of old stone and wood. A
tall man, dressed in a grey suit, strode down the front
steps of the building.

"Welcome to Tuskegee!"

Booker T. Washington's handshake was as strong
as his deep voice. His sturdy body stood like a tree—
solid and powerful. Hoping to match his impressive
posture, I thrust my own narrow shoulders back. Mr.
Washington stood three inches taller than my own six
feet.

For a few minutes we exchanged pleasant conversation. As we did so I gazed around at the Tuskegee
campus. I had never seen anything like it. There was
yellow soil and red and purple and brown. The colored soil was in bands in the banks. I saw all sorts of
things except grass or plants. There were erosion gul-
lies in which an ox could fall and get lost! Gone were
the handsome landscapes, the proud buildings, the thriv-
ing bushes, and lush gardens of Iowa State.

A nearby sign identified the building we were standing before as the Administration Building. I grew eager
to visit the school's laboratory. "President Washington, could you take me to the laboratory now?" I asked.

"We're proud of what our students have done here at Tuskegee," said Dr. Washington. "I want you to see our Agricultural Hall. Every inch of that building was built by students."

"They sound like a most energetic group," I agreed. "But if first we could visit the lab and see . . ."

"Energetic! Yes, that's the perfect word for them!" Dr. Washington's eyes sparkled with pride. "This campus would have nothing if it were not for our energetic students. Oh, and our instructors, too. Side by side they have laid bricks, pounded nails, painted walls . . ."

As Dr. Washington continued talking, I remembered an old story President Abraham Lincoln told people. "If a person wants to talk about hens, but doesn't have any to talk about, he might talk about eggs. The listener who wants to share talk about hens may think he's talking about hens. The subject is close enough to fool most people."

Two more times I asked about the lab at Tuskegee. Two more times Dr. Washington told me about the "eager and wonderful students I would be working with here." I smiled knowingly as Dr. Washington kept talking.

". . . and I believe we can accomplish anything here, as long as we work together," he continued.

I nodded. "It will not matter where we build our lab on the campus," I said. "There is no danger of destroying any of nature's growing treasures."

"None at all," Dr. Washington answered, grateful that I understood. "I knew you were just the man to build our laboratory. Why, did you know there's a story that you can even grow corn . . ."

". . . on a wood floor?" I interrupted. "I did not

know that tale had traveled so far. Please do not ask me to do that."

Dr. Washington laughed, "Ill be quite satisfied with a laboratory!"

I was led to a one-room apartment on the campus. It was pleasantly furnished with a bed, a stuffed chair, and corner table. After an enjoyable dinner with Dr. Washington, I set out alone to explore the Tuskegee campus by evening.

The moonlight added no beauty to the scene viewed that afternoon. How often I had walked the Iowa State campus and enjoyed the rich fresh breezes through the blossoms and trees. There were no such winds here. The air was stale and heavy. My steps slowed as gloom and disappointment took over.

Suddenly the figure of a young man approached. "Evenin', sir," the lad spoke cheerfully. "Nice night for a walk. Beautiful night, I'd say."

Before I could reply, he was gone. I stopped and stood, listening as his footsteps disappeared. How happy the lad sounded. What a happy spirit he carried.

A sense of shame quickly crowded out the disappointment and gloom I had felt. Truly, it was not for man to measure beauty and joy on the surface. It lies within—inside the hearts and souls of people. Why should I feel sadness for what *I* had given up?

A vivid picture came to my mind—the picture of a lone man walking through a garden. How tragic that vision of Jesus, betrayed and tortured by emptiness in the Garden of Gethsemane. Yes, that was cause for sorrow and sadness. How ashamed I felt.

As I continued walking, my steps quickened. I felt

refreshed, like a new life had come to my spirit. Once more the Lord had lightened my load and given me strength. Somehow I knew He had brought me to this place.

Two days later, I stood before my first class. There were twelve students sitting on the tired benches in Agricultural Hall. There was a blackboard without chalk, a teacher's desk without a chair, and three windows with no shades to keep the glaring sun from beating in on my students. But it was their words that caused me the greatest concern.

"We don't want to learn about no crop raisin'," one large boy told me quickly. "Our pappies was slaves and their pappies, too. We ain't wantin' to do that."

There was a chorus of agreeing mumbles.

"Let the white folks get their hands dirty!" shouted a boy from the back of the room. His patched overalls were faded and thin. "Let us learn somethin' that can keep our hands clean."

Again the heads nodded.

"We wants to learn a trade," said another. He wore a hand-me-down shirt torn on one shoulder. "Anybody can farm."

The words were bitter. Yet, as I looked at the students I understood. These young men were children of slaves. Their parents had sacrificed and worked to send them to Tuskegee. Now, as I looked into their eyes, I saw a great hunger for knowledge. The appetite was there, and it was my job to satisfy it.

"You have said that anybody can farm," I began, my gaze moving from face to face among the dozen men before me. "You have farmed, your fathers and mothers have farmed, and their parents before them. You

say you did not come here to learn farming. Well, I did
not come here to teach farming either."

A few of the students exchanged puzzled looks. But
they listened to every word.

"I've come to offer you a partnership. Together we
will work with the Lord in exploring all He has given
us. His fantastic world holds countless secrets. We need
to learn the mysteries of the soil, the rain, the sun. We
will fight wars—against diseases and bugs. Too often
we have gone hungry because there were no solutions
to the mysteries of our world. If we work together as
partners, we may bring new strength to our people and
a new life to our land."

One boy in a front seat shook his head. "You make
it all sound so good, like a big adventure or somethin'.
It's work! You must not have been around these parts
much. You can't grow much of anything around here."

"You're right," I answered. "It will take work— lots
of work. But as to what will grow around here, we
don't really know. We have never tried much besides
cotton. Once we get a lab, we can test the soil. Maybe
we can find other plants that will grow here. We are
not farmers. We are detectives."

"You talk about a lab," came a shout from a boy in a
tattered shirt. "We ain't got no lab here at Tuskegee.
How we goin' solve all these mysteries you're talkin'
about without a lab?"

How glad I was for that question! I prayed quickly
for the Lord's forgiveness. Like a spider, I had lured
an insect into my web. I hoped my motives would make
up for my sneaky weaving.

"You're right, my friend. We have no lab. But we
can have one. It's up to you. Today we begin a treasure

hunt, the likes of which you will never see again."

All eyes were on me. Everyone was listening.

"We'll go into town and knock on every door. When the door is opened, we will explain we are students at Tuskegee Institute putting together a laboratory. Any pan or pot, any jar or old lamp, any container at all, we would be grateful to accept. Dishes, jugs, bottles, and cans."

"What if they're dirty?" asked a boy in the back.

"We will clean them," I answered. "Refuse nothing. Tell your parents, your friends, everyone you know. We will sort through scrap and trash. The treasure we seek may be anywhere."

The idea seemed to catch fire. Maybe these students were ready for a challenge right at this time in their lives. Anyway, the search had started.

In the weeks that followed, my classroom in Agricultural Hall looked like a giant junkyard. But what wonderful junk it was! In bags and boxes, on carts and wagons, my eager students brought in their findings. Jars and bottles lined the walls. A tower of saucepans stood stacked in the corner.

"Look what I've got, sir!" one of the boys shouted one day. He carried a handsome lantern, its chimney still shining. "We can use this, can't we?"

"We sure can!" I answered. "With a little work, it can be made into a heater for test tubes and beakers. It's wonderful!"

The boy smiled, hauling the lantern into the room.

When Dr. Washington stopped by, his expression was of curious confusion. He said little, but only walked among the students who were scraping and scouring our latest collections. One afternoon, as he was making a visit, one of the boys came running in with a big bushelbasket.

"They're rubber patches," he shouted, plopping the basket in the middle of the room. "My cousin brought them over from Atlanta just for us."

I glanced at Dr. Washington. His eyebrows were raised in amused puzzlement. I could tell he had no idea what we were doing, but he trusted that I did.

"Don't worry," I told him. "You will be surprised at what can come from all of this."

Dr. Washington smiled, nodded, and walked away without saying a word.

Once we had our laboratory equipment, we next needed a plot of soil. It was time to find out just what could be grown in the land around us. We needed to test the soil to see how rich it was. I asked Dr. Washington for some land to farm.

A few days later Dr. Washington again came to my classroom.

"I have your land," he said. "Bring your students, and I will show you where it is."

Eagerly our small group followed Dr. Washington outside. Minutes later we stood looking at a large plot of land. The sight was unbelievable! Large mounds of old rubbish dotted the area. Among these piles stood huge hungry hogs. The land was covered with wild weeds.

"It's about twenty acres," Dr. Washington explained. "It doesn't look like much, but I know you will be able to do a lot with it."

I shook my head, still amazed at the sight before me. One curly-tailed grey hog tugged at a giant weed. Finally, the weed gave up. Happily the hog chomped on his feast.

"Well, at least we know some things can grow on this soil," I mumbled to President Washington. "I only hope we can raise more than weeds."

I felt my friend's strong and gentle hand on my shoulder. "Don't worry," he said, a trace of chuckle in his voice. "You will be surprised at what can come from all of this."

How familiar those words sounded as he repeated my advice to him. As Dr. Washington walked away, I smiled myself.

Suddenly the hog I had noticed before let out a wild squeal. I turned to watch him swallow the last of his supper.

"Whe-he-eee!" the hog squealed again. He stood watching us.

My students looked at one another, not knowing what to say or do.

"Come on!" I ordered. "He's telling us to get to work. We've got a lot to do!"

Secrets of the Soil

In time I knew we'd be doing the impossible with our Tuskegee land. But first our twenty-acre plot had to be cleared of weeds and rubbish. Each day my students worked until their backs ached and their muscles begged for mercy. When the land was clear, I had a surprise waiting for the class.

"You see before you a two-horse plow, ready to be put into operation," I said. One of the horses whinnied in the morning sunlight, slapping at a fly on his back with his tail.

"I never did see a two-horse plow," one of the students said, walking around the team of horses. "Everybody here uses just one horse." He shook his head in amazement.

"Who can use it?" another boy asked. "None of us have driven a two-horse plow."

Taking my place behind the team of horses and plow, I smiled. "Step aside, my friends, I have work to do."

Slowly the horses stepped forward as I snapped the reins. The steel blade of the plow slid into the soil,

turning it aside as we moved ahead. Like hungry foxes on a rabbit's trail, my students followed me across the plot of land. On our return, we found two farmers watching us.

"Hey, ain't you the professor here—that Carver fellow?" one asked

"That's who I am," I answered.

"Then what you doin' drivin' a plow?"

I smiled. "I know of no law, the Lord's or man's, that says I can't. Do you?"

The two men exchanged puzzled looks. "No, I guess not," came an answer.

"This soil turning will be taking us most of the day," I said. "If you care to watch us, feel free. Get your friends, too."

My invitation was like throwing corn to crows. Off the men went, only to return a while later with six more farmers. The idea of a professor plowing a field seemed quite a fine joke. The laughter rolled across the field like happy music.

"Hope you're not planning to raise anything on this no good land," came one loud shout. " 'Cepting weeds. Yeah, I guess you can get the best weeds in Alabama on this soil."

There was much truth in the farmer's words, and I couldn't help smiling. The hard clay soil rolled to the side of the plow. How I missed the deep richness of Iowa soil.

And yet this red soil offered a challenge, and I meant to find the soil's secret. Surely it could be enriched. I glanced at the farmers watching me. Their faces were curious, reflecting their interest in my work. I had wanted them to come here. They could see what a two-horse plow could do. If a Tuskegee teacher could turn the soil, surely they could too. At least I hoped that was what they were thinking. And if a useful crop could be grown here, could these same farmers not make their own lands richer?

Once the soil was turned, my students were ready for the next step.

"I'm turning you loose again," I told them one morning. "Just like I did when we needed a lab. This time I want you to visit the woods. Gather the mold off the leaves. Go into the swamps and creeks. Bring back buckets of mud and muck. Head to the barns and bring back the animal droppings."

"But why?" one student asked, with an astonished look. He obviously thought I had gone mad in the hot sun.

"We must put new nourishment into our land. The things you are to collect will make the soil rich," I answered. "All of us must help."

In the next week, our twenty-acre plot became a dumping ground. I taught the students how to use the two-horse plow. Day after day we turned the clay soil with the buckets of waste brought in. The dirt began to look darker and richer.

We put our handmade lab equipment to work testing the soil. A heavy kitchen cup was our mortar, a container for grinding up substances. A flat piece of iron served as a pestle. Our materials were crude, but they worked!

I knew my students had only one crop in mind—cotton. Yet it was clear that the constant growing of cotton on our land, and land throughout the South, had robbed the soil of nutrients. The dirt had lost its power to nourish. Like the thieves in the temples, we had stolen the wealth of the soil that the Lord had provided. Now we had to enrich it again.

When the day for planting arrived, my students came early to our plot.

"Let us bow our heads and ask for the good Lord's blessing on our first crop here," I said.

One of the students, Ambrose Lee Harper, stepped forward. "Yes, let's ask the Lord to bring us the best twenty acres of cotton in all the Southland."

I shook my head. "The Lord can do anything," I said, "but I think it is asking too much to grow cotton from the seeds of cowpeas."

Puzzled and surprised, my students did not know what to say. Ambrose Lee moved toward me, his eyes angry.

"We have cleared this land and mixed the soil to grow cowpeas? Cowpeas is a worthless crop. We thought we was workin' to grow cotton. You fooled us, Mister Carver."

"I'm sorry, Ambrose Lee. But I know this soil is not right for raising good cotton. It needs refreshing and enriching. A good crop of cowpeas will feed nutrients into the soil. Perhaps then, we may think about cotton."

Ambrose Lee was not convinced. He turned and walked away. Suddenly he whirled around and shook his fist.

"You're all fools, raisin' cowpeas! Mister Carver, you're the biggest fool of all!"

As I looked to the rest of the students, I wondered how many of them felt the same. Maybe it would be better to plant cotton and to have them all see it would not grow. Would the students learn more? Perhaps. Yet it was wrong to waste the soil. Or was I wrong?

Doubts. More doubts. Sometimes my whole mind was filled with doubts. Was I truly following the path the Lord had chosen for me? Sometimes the urge to paint returned. Other times, when I visited students at the Tuskegee dormitory, I sat down at the piano and began to play. In my thoughts, I recalled those happy days at Simpson College. Maybe I was meant to be an artist—or pianist. Had I missed the Lord's directions?

Maybe Ambrose Lee was right. Perhaps I was a fool. And if I was a fool, what business did I have leading others as their teacher?

As the cowpeas crept up through the soil into the sunlight, we kept the soil free from weeds. And daily in the lab, we kept adding equipment. Carefully we cut the tops off bottles to make beakers. We made an alcohol lamp from an old ink bottle by adding a wick from twisted plant fibers.

"You don't throw anything away, do you?" my students asked often.

I smiled. "Everything has a use," I answered. "It's finding the use that is exciting."

When it came time to harvest the crop of cowpeas, I found little joy among my students. If they saw any use or excitement in the rows of vegetable stalks, these young farmers kept it well hidden. Slowly they wandered among the cowpeas, picking the peas from each weary stalk.

"Never thought I'd be pickin' cowpeas when I came here to Tuskegee," one boy mumbled. "I guess Ambrose Lee was right."

"Well, the soil may be better now," grunted another student, "but I sure hate the sight of these cowpeas."

"They don't seem ugly when you eat them," I answered. "Come to the campus cafeteria tomorrow night at seven o'clock. Bring your best appetites."

Once more my students looked bewildered. But they agreed to come.

The pots and pans rattled that Saturday afternoon. I boiled the brown peas, sprinkling in salt and mixing them with several hunks of fresh pork. By seven o'clock the table was set, my guests were seated, and I served the food.

"Must we eat these cowpeas?" one boy asked, his face revealing his distaste for the idea. "Cowpeas is livestock food, not people food."

Spooning a serving onto his plate, I smiled. "Let's wait and give them a chance."

There were few words spoken around the table for a little while. I stole glances from face to face. Finally, one student spoke.

"Delicious! This is the best meal I ever ate!"

Another head nodded. "Just what I was thinking! But I thought I must be wrong. How could those miserable little cowpeas taste so good?"

The eager happy eaters gulped down helping after helping. Soon every plate was scraped clean. There was not one cowpea left!

"Say, maybe we should plant cowpeas again," some suggested.

I shook my head. "No, don't let your stomachs do your thinking. These cowpeas put fresh nutrients back into the soil. Now I'm thinking we could raise a hearty crop of sweet potatoes. They're good eating for men and livestock. We can make starch from them. What we don't use now, we can dry out and have for hungry times later. We should be able to raise about eighty bushels an acre."

The eyes around the table widened. I knew what they were thinking. Fifty bushels in this part of the South was about average. Sixty bushels of sweet potatoes was a healthy harvest. Seventy was unbelievable. But eighty bushels an acre was impossible!

Yet no one challenged my words. A few of my students exchanged surprised looks. Still there were no outward challenges. Perhaps the cowpeas had helped me win an important victory. My students were willing to trust me.

And if they were willing to help me raise the sweet potatoes, we could then plant cotton. The soil would be rich and full of the nutrients needed for the cotton.

"Come on, Professor Carver," one student called out. "Let's find a piano and see if you still play as well as you cook."

"Only if you sing while I play," I agreed.

In minutes we were gathered around an old piano in the dormitory. Thankfully, the loud voices of my students drowned out the mistakes of their pianist.

Praise the harvest, praise the home;
Praise the Lord, where e'er we roam . . .

Across the Tuskegee campus the music drifted.

Unknown to us then, a lone figure was strolling slowly along a pathway. President Booker T. Washington was struggling with a big problem that prevented him from sleeping.

Soon that problem would be troubling me, too.

School on Wheels

Everything at Tuskegee seemed to be going well. Our twenty acres provided 1600 bushels of sweet potatoes—eighty bushels an acre. My students were proud, even overjoyed.

Eagerly we began planting the "King Crop"—cotton. The tired, sandy clay had become deep, dark, rich soil. It turned casily as we plowed and planted. In a few weeks, the hearty stalks grew straight and full of blossoms in the sun.

"We are grateful to You, Oh Lord," I prayed nightly. "Without You, we are nothing."

Harvest proved the happiest time of all. Each acre produced a five hundred pound bale of cotton, compared to the two hundred pounds each one had provided before.

But with my joy, I still felt a hurt inside. Each time I saw our leader, Booker T. Washington, I sensed that he was a troubled man. Within his eyes I saw sadness. But the cause of his worry remained a mystery to me.

My worry for my friend was pushed aside by new

tasks at Tuskegee. Often I walked by myself into the Alabama countryside. Never had I seen so many kinds of trees! Giant oak, sturdy pine, spreading spruce—twenty-two varieties of hardwood species. I shared my discoveries on paper, writing nature articles for magazines and newspapers. Farmers wrote me questions about the soil, their crops, and all the land around them. Eagerly I answered their letters, hoping they would take good care of the riches the Lord had provided.

Early one morning I slowly walked through a swampy marsh near the Tuskegee campus. I gazed skyward. Spanish moss draped lazily over the branches of sweet gum trees like giant spider webs. Only narrow streaks of sunlight peeked through.

Suddenly I stumbled. My hands flung forward into the sticky mud. Pulling myself up, I jerked a handkerchief from my pocket. I rubbed my muddy hands into the cloth. A few yards away I saw a large puddle of water. Quickly I walked to it, dipped my handkerchief in, and continued rubbing my hands.

The swamp mud came off easily. But I noticed that my white handkerchief was now bright blue. Yes, it was as blue as the sky on a cloudless day. I held the cloth up into a sliver of sunlight. The blue looked even brighter.

My heartbeat quickened. Still clenching the handkerchief tightly, I hurried back to the lab on the campus.

From a bucket in the corner, I took a large clump of red clay. Carefully I set it on a tray and poured water over it. The sand and grit washed away. A sticky red paste remained. I pressed my finger into it, then drew a line across a piece of paper nearby. Holding the paper close to the window, I smiled.

"Paint. There is paint in the clay. Blue. Red. Look at that color!" It was hard to control my excitement. Once the clay was washed clean, heated into powder, and mixed with liquid, people could have paint. They could paint their homes, their barns, their churches, anything they wanted.

Once more I knew the Lord had spoken. There seemed to be no end to His gifts. I did not mind that He had pushed me to the ground to find this gift.

President Booker T. Washington shared my joy of discovery. "You continue to bring attention to Tuskegee, while bringing respect to our Negro people," he said. "I am glad you are here, Professor Carver."

I was glad I had come to Tuskegee, too. And yet, I still longed to share the troubles he carried—to ease his burden.

Finally, late one night as I walked alone across the campus my chance came.

Moonlight covered the campus like a silver fog. It painted a shiny surface on the new red brick buildings that dotted the grounds of Tuskegee. As I returned from visiting the students in their dormitory I heard footsteps behind me. Unlike the quick, steady movement of younger people, these steps were slow, almost plodding. I turned to see the familiar outline of Dr. Washington approaching.

"Making sure the buildings are all locked up?" I called.

Dr. Washington chuckled as he moved closer. "I'm taking a midnight walk. Sometimes sleep does not come so easily to me."

No words were spoken for several minutes as we walked together. Finally, Dr. Washington stopped. "Are you happy here?"

"At Tuskegee, sir? I am happier than I have ever been. You have built a fine school here."

There was another long pause.

"But does it ever trouble you that we are here in such a small world?" he asked gently. "Yes, I am proud of Tuskegee. The students who come here take much away. But think of all the young people who cannot come, who still suffer to live through each day. Somehow I feel we are failing them."

"Failing." How tragic and sad that word sounded. "In what way?" I asked.

"We have worked hard to teach our people to raise good crops in order to improve their farms and homes." President Washington's voice sounded strained and tired. "But we reach so few. If only we could bring all our people here to Tuskegee . . ."

"We reach all we can," I interrupted.

"Yes," he agreed. "But for each black man we help there are ten thousand still untouched. Each time I travel I see them. How I wish we might bring them here and help them."

So that was the mystery, the problem that had troubled my friend for so long. He not only carried the worries of his own students here at Tuskegee, but he carried the plight of our whole race.

A shame swept over me. My life had become so busy that, for a time, I had forgotten my main reason for coming to Tuskegee. I, too, should have been carrying my friend's concern for our people.

It was not that I was blind to the world around me.

I had seen the beaten, drab cabins sprinkled everywhere in the South. Inside these one- and two-room grey shacks with holes in the walls there often lived ten or twelve members of one family. The bed was often a dirt floor, with creek drinking water being shared with pigs and livestock.

"In time, we will reach more people," I told Dr. Washington.

He nodded. "I suppose. But how painful the waiting is. How long they suffer." He turned, "Good night."

Watching the man slowly walk away my heart was heavy. How much he had done, how hard he had worked. It seemed so unfair that he carried such a burden.

Sleep did not come easily for me that night. The hours dragged by. Dr. Washington's words lingered in my mind. "How I wish we might bring them here and help them . . ."

Suddenly I sat up in bed. "That's it!" I exclaimed, jumping out of bed. "We'll go to them!"

By the time Dr. Washington came to his office the next morning, I had been waiting there for an hour. I could not control my enthusiasm.

"Our people cannot come to Tuskegee," I exclaimed, "but we can go to them!"

Dr. Washington looked confused. "We cannot carry buildings on our back, George. Maybe you had best . . ."

"No, we need not carry buildings," I interrupted. "But we can carry our knowledge and our tools. We can put a butter churn and a milk tester on a wagon. We can load some garden tools—the newest and most modern. Carry a new plow . . ."

President Washington's eyes sparkled and a happy

smile replaced the worried wrinkles I had seen for so long. He liked the idea! He really like it!

"... and we can go out in the countryside. We can take Tuskegee right to their doorstep," I added.

"It—it all sounds so fantastic," President Washington exclaimed. "Could it really be done?"

I nodded eagerly. "We can try it. I'll go out on weekends so I can stay in my classroom during the week."

"Let's do try it, George. Let's show our people a better way to farm."

Our planning started at once and it caught fire like dry grass. A man from the North offered money for the wagon. Invitations poured in from area farmers.

"We hear you are going to be helping farmers," wrote one man. "I have forty acres you may use for anything you wish."

"I have read all your articles in the magazines," wrote another farmer. "Mister Carver, I believe you can do anything with the soil. Please come."

Carefully, we planned the wagon and bought the equipment. A cream separator was added to our original list. We bought a new spike-toothed harrow and a diverse cultivator for breaking up hard soil.

Finally, our 'school on wheels' was ready to go. I picked one of my best students to go with me on the first trip. Early one June morning in 1906, Tom Campbell and I set forth. With a snap of the reins, our horse-drawn wagon jerked forward. The other members from my class cheered and shouted.

"Teach them good, fellows!" one student yelled. "Show them what we can do!"

"We'll try!" I hollered back through our dust.

The wagon bounced and bumped along the rutted

road. Tom kept a careful watch over our equipment on the back of the wagon. We didn't want to lose a single tool.

Within an hour we reached our destination. A run-down cabin sat at the base of a hillside about a mile outside the town of Chechow. A small collection of farmers stood outside. One of them ran forward.

"Doctor Carver, it's you!" A black man with grey-white whiskers helped me off the wagon. The other farmers grouped around us.

"Can we get started at once?" I asked. "Does anyone have a strong horse?"

It seemed the farmers were as eager as we were. One man ran off, returning minutes later with a muscled field horse. Quickly we hitched him to our steel-beam plow and began our work.

"When your farmland slopes, you must follow its natural contour," I explained. "Never plow in a straight line, uphill and down. By following the curve of the hill, the water will not run off so fast, carrying the precious topsoil away."

How closely all the men listened. They watched every move Tom and I made as we worked. I only wished Dr. Washington could have been there.

Once the field was plowed, we turned to other matters. We showed the farmers how to fight insects and diseases of trees and bushes and how to plant useful gardens.

Our program turned also to the wives of the farmers. We showed the womenfolk the best ways to cook their meals and to clean. Curtains were made from flour sacks and rugs were woven from corn shucks and grasses.

Everywhere we went we were welcomed. Our school on wheels was a big success!

"Please come to our town," wrote one mayor. "You may give classes in our town hall, the church, or anywhere you wish. Just come!"

And so we traveled. Soon Tom took over the wagon himself so I could remain at Tuskegee.

Other students joined him and we added women to the staff, too!

The months slipped into years. More buildings sprang up on the Tuskegee campus and my classes grew larger.

Once more cotton grew thick and proudly over the Alabama countryside. Farmers looked with pride at their great yields—their hearty crops.

And yet, one night I awakened with damp sweat coating my body. Over and over a Biblical passage pounded itself into my mind. It was a warning from Proverbs 27: "Boast not thyself of tomorrow; for thou knowest not what a day may bring forth."

As I lay back on my pillow, the words stayed with me. Somehow I knew the Lord was sharing a fear with me—a fear that would bring much sorrow to our people.

But even in my worst dreams, I could not have foreseen the trouble that lay ahead.

Fighting a Killer

The South was a wonderland of white. Everywhere the cotton bloomed rich and pure in the afternoon sun. I listened to the farmers boast of their fine crops, their huge yields.

The world was almost perfect.

Almost.

And then came the killer.

A person would never think the boll weevil was dangerous by looking at it. Barely a quarter inch long, this black bug appears harmless. But it is really a vicious killer.

Boll weevils eat only the white cotton ball. They feast on the bud blossoms in the summer. When the cold autumn winds arrive, the weevils slip into the ground or empty plant pods. As the young cotton plants sprout in early spring, the mother weevil lays her eggs. In three days, the eggs hatch into hungry baby grubs. The grubs eat the new buds, then spin a kind of cocoon. After a brief sleep, the grubs emerge as full-grown weevils, eager to eat more cotton.

In 1902, we learned the Texas cotton crops had been attacked by the murdering bugs. I shared the news in the articles I wrote about farming for Alabama newspapers. When I spoke to farmers at their meetings, I offered a warning.

"You must rest your fields at times," I said, "rotating them by planting different crops or planting none at all. Some crops rob the soil by stealing all its nitrates—its richness. After harvesting such a crop, you should plant a different crop, a crop that will give the soil a chance to replenish its own richness. Better yet, allow the soil to rest, like we rest, when we have worked hard."

There were murmurs in the audience. Some farmers nodded agreement, while others were not convinced.

"And we cannot depend only on one crop like cotton," I continued. "The boll weevil is headed this way. It may be years before the weevils arrive, but we must be ready. If we have crops other than cotton in our fields, this killer will be stopped. If we have only cotton, it will feast like a king."

Harsh grumbles could be heard. The cotton fields were too rich, too full. No one wanted to think about growing anything but cotton. Good money came from the sale of cotton.

Slowly the killer bug chewed its way across the South. When the weevils crossed from Texas into Louisiana, I increased my warnings.

"The cotton fields of Louisiana are a wasteland," I wrote in my columns. "Ours will be too, if we do not stand ready. Plant sweet potatoes. Plant peanuts. These crops help rebuild the soil, and they are fine nourishment to man. The boll weevil will not touch sweet potatoes or peanuts."

One night I spoke before a group of white farm owners about twenty miles from Tuskegee. They had invited me, but I sensed I was a mite unwelcome. The sunburned red faces in the audience looked angry and mean. The air hung heavy with unhappy grumbling.

I had barely started to speak when one farmer in the front row stood up and shook his finger at me. "You been writin' in the newspaper that we should stop growin' cotton. Did you happen to look around you as you came over here tonight?"

I nodded.

"Then you saw cotton, Mr. Professor, lots of cotton. Growin' fine all over."

"Right now it is," I answered. "But for how long? You may have also read that the boll weevil is coming our way. Louisiana, Mississippi, and then us. Don't you see . . ."

Another voice shouted from the back of the group.

"I see a fancy teacher trying to get us to give up the best and only crop that can grow around here. If we give up cotton, how do we feed our families? Cotton sells for cash—fast."

"You can raise other crops. Take sweet potatoes. You can eat them, your livestock can eat them. You can make starch from them. You can . . ."

"And goobers?" the first man interrupted. "I suppose we can feed our families on goobers?"

"Goobers." The nickname that farmers gave peanuts often made me smile. But in this tense crowd, I found myself not smiling.

"Peanuts enrich the soil, and they enrich our bodies," I said. "They are cheap to raise and give us more food value than any other legume. They grow in pods underground—protected against killer bugs."

"Well, you can raise all the goobers you want," the first man shouted, shaking his fist at me. "I'll keep raising cotton. You can dig the goobers."

Quickly the man strode out of the room. Chairs scraped as other men stood to go. In minutes I was alone in the small town hall. With a sad spirit, I headed back to Tuskegee. They would not listen to my warnings. Doom was near.

My carriage bumped and rolled along the dirt road back to Tuskegee. Lights in the farmhouses looked like tiny fireflies in the blackness. Night bugs sang their happy songs. If only the peacefulness of this night could remain. But it was not to be.

Like a starved villain, the boll weevil attacked.

Billions of the vicious beetles swept across the cotton fields in 1914. Proud blossoms became empty shells, ravaged by the monster bugs.

We had planted our acres at Tuskegee College in peanuts. In the midst of the deadly decay of cotton plants, our peanut vines stood fresh and strong.

"You were right, Dr. Carver," one of my students said, as we walked among the green leaves. "The boll weevils have done no damage to our peanut plants. Everything you said was true."

The words offered little comfort. "There is no joy in being right when around you there is nothing but suffering," I said.

The next morning, as I stood before my class of students, there was a rumbling of voices outside my door. Moments later a lone thin man stepped inside. He held a cap in his hand and turned it over and over.

"Mister Carver, sir. We've come to see you. We—we need you. Our crops are gone. We don't—we don't know what to do. Please—please . . ." The poor man's voice broke, unable to go on. My heart wept for the man. Quickly I walked to him.

"I will do all I can," I answered. "My students and everyone here at Tuskegee will help."

Quickly we set up a meeting. All the cotton farmers were invited. The largest meeting room in Agricultural Hall was crowded. Everywhere I looked I saw the same sad, tragic faces.

President Washington welcomed the people. How much I admired that man. He was always a man of business, calm and organized. His carefully tailored clothes lent stature to his powerful manner.

For a moment I felt ashamed of my own appearance. The tired coat and trousers I wore had seen fifteen years of service. The worn cornhusk tie did little to help. With my drooping shoulders and bony, tall frame, I probably resembled a prize scarecrow.

Suddenly I felt foolish. This was not a meeting to look at clothes. This was a meeting to save lives. As President Washington introduced me and stepped aside, I took the speaker's stand willingly.

"Friends, you wear faces that show your sorrow and grief. We all mourn the death of good crops."

I looked from side to side as I gripped the wooden stand.

"But now the mourning time is over. It is a time for action. There is work to be done."

"Our crops lie worthless in the fields," yelled someone from the back of the room. "We are all ruined."

I shook my head. "No, no, no. True, the cotton is gone. You must plow it under the soil. Spray the soil with poison to kill the deadly weevil. And then plant peanuts."

"Peanuts!" A man in the front row shook his head wearily. "We feed peanuts to hogs and monkeys. Now we must raise them for ourselves?"

"Yes," I snapped back, somewhat surprised at my own sharp voice. "The peanut is a fine food for man. We can thank the good Lord for peanuts."

A large man in the middle of the room stood up. "We should listen to this man. We should have listened before. If he says to plant peanuts, I will plant peanuts! And perhaps if we treat him kindly, he will share his wisdom with us further."

I smiled and nodded. "I promise to do all I can."

As soon as the meeting was over I hurried to my room. At once I began to write. All night long I wrote. By the next day, the job was done. Quickly my bulletin went out to the farmers. Carefully I explained how to plant and harvest the peanut.

But most importantly, I shared the uses I had discovered for the peanut crop:

1. Like all other members of the pod-bearing family, they enrich the soil.
2. They are easily and cheaply grown.
3. For humans, the nuts possess a wider range of food values than any other legume.
4. The nutritional value of the peanut vines as a stock food compares favorably with that of the cowpea.
5. They are easy to plant, easy to grow, and easy to harvest . . .

On and on the list went. Letters poured in from farmers across the South. Wherever I went farmers wanted to share their excitement about the peanut.

"I couldn't believe it when you said we could raise two crops of those goobers every year," one man wrote. "All these years we've been laughin' at the things. Now they're going to keep us from starving."

One man rode his old wagon a full fifty miles just to say thanks in person. He was a giant of a fellow with a full set of red whiskers that looked like blazing fire in the afternoon sun.

"Nobody would have thought those tiny peanuts could be so good for a man's body," the visitor said. "It just don't seem possible that a pound of peanuts could provide more nutrition and energy than a whole pound of choice sirloin steak."

"But it's true," I answered. "Mix peanuts with corn and feed the mixture to your pigs before butchering. You'll find the quality of your pork will improve. Peanuts are good medicine for both man *and* beast."

Farmers weren't the only ones happy about the new peanut discoveries. Bakers and candy-makers were excited too. After the oil was removed from the peanuts, the clean cake that remained could be mixed easily with flour and meal.

"It makes a wonderful ice cream," wrote one man.

I was pleased with the reception given my discoveries. But close to home, in Tuskegee, some people were still not convinced of the peanut's value.

A teaching friend approached me one morning. He held the bulletin I had sent out about peanuts in his hand.

"It all *sounds* good on paper," he said. "But does the peanut really *taste* good?"

I smiled and nodded. "So we have a doubting Thomas right here in Tuskegee, do we? Pass the word along. If any teachers would like a complete peanut meal, they may visit the school cafeteria tomorrow for luncheon."

My friend's mouth dropped open in surprise. "A-a luncheon of peanuts?"

"Promptly at noon," I said, enjoying his disbelief.

Once more I rattled the pots and pans in the Tuskegee cafeteria. First, it was having to prove the value of cowpeas to students. Now, my fellow teachers needed convincing about peanuts.

People clustered around the main table in the

cafeteria by twelve o'clock. It would seem there was more than one doubting Thomas among our Tuskegee group.

We began the meal with peanut soup, a smooth but tangy broth. Next there was mock chicken, salad, ice cream, and a coffee-type drink, together with a variety of cookies and candy. It all came from the mighty peanuts grown on our own college soil. As my guests finished their five course luncheon, one large teacher stood and lifted his water glass.

"I propose a toast," he called out. "To our fellow worker, George Washington Carver, who has proven that even fat stomachs like mine can be richly filled with tiny peanuts."

My friends clapped and raised their water glasses.

"Thank you," I answered, "and I promise you there is no trace of peanuts in your water."

Laughter shook the cafeteria.

I was glad the Lord had shown me the miracles in His creation—the peanut. God was good to me.

Farmers followed my instructions. They plowed their cotton under and sprayed poison on the soil. A month later, they planted their new crop—peanuts. Soon the countryside was carpeted in green vines. "Goobers" were planted everywhere.

While the farmers worked in their fields, I worked in my laboratory. All the foods that could come from the peanuts even amazed me—cheese, candies, peanut bread, sausage—the list seemed endless.

The peanut fields seemed endless. Green and healthy, the vines stretched across the farms of the South. The farmers had taken my advice. Peanut crops were everywhere.

As I walked home late one night from a meeting,

I heard the rustle of bushes ahead of me. Moonlight revealed a shadowy figure blocking my path.
I slowed my steps, but continued walking.

"Carver—is that you, Carver?" The voice was
harsh and threatening.

"Yes," I answered. "My name is Carver."

The figure approached until the man's face was
only a few inches from mine. I could smell liquor
on his breath.

"You ruined me, nigger. I planted peanuts like
you said. Then I harvested them like you said. Now
nobody wants them. Nobody!" he shouted.

The stranger raised his hand, ready to strike. But
something held me firm. I could not move. "But-
but did you ship your peanuts North? Did you . . ."

Angrily the man grabbed the front of my coat.
"Yes, I did just that," he hissed. "But they don't

want my peanuts, nigger. They got all they want—
and then some."

My mind was whirling. I almost wished the
stranger would hit me so his words might be dulled.
But he did not strike. Mumbling and half-sobbing,
the man released my coat and turned away. Slowly
he staggered off into the darkness.

For several moments I could not move. The im-
pact of the man's words rushed through my mind.
Was this going to happen to other farmers? Had
they taken my advice, only to find themselves with
crops they could not market?

My answer came all too soon. In the days that
followed, I heard countless stories of peanuts harvested, with no buyers. What a fool I had been!
Why had I only seen half the problem? I had found
a crop to grow but nothing to do with it. The products I had invented in the lab had not yet been accepted by businessmen or produced for the mar-
ketplace. The ideas were there, but ideas weren't
enough.

"You're the biggest fool of all, Mister Carver!"
The words of Ambrose Lee Harper haunted me.

I retreated into my lab. Only there could I avoid
the faces of my students and friends. Only there
could I be alone.

But somehow I knew I was *not* alone. Even in
the silence and stillness I felt another presence.
Falling to my knees, I begged forgiveness and un-
derstanding from my Savior and Creator.

And as I prayed, I was drawn to my feet. Out of
the lab I went into the nearby woodlands and fields.
The sun warmed my skin. The soft breezes refreshed
my body.

"Oh, Dear Creator," I asked softly, "why did You make this Universe?"

A wind stirred the trees a bit, and I seemed to hear a voice, "Your little mind asks too much," came the answer. "Ask something more your size."

Confused, I rubbed my chin. "What was man made for?" I whispered.

Once more, the voice came, "You are still asking too much. Try once more."

I fell to my knees. "Dear Lord, why did You make the peanut?"

Once more the breezes rustled through the trees. "Now you are asking questions your own size, and I can reveal the answers."

Quickly I sprang to my feet. Not wasting a moment I ran back to the campus. Two of my students stood whispering outside the lab door.

"Bring me peanuts—please bring me all the peanuts you can carry," I ordered. "And hurry!"

The two exchanged puzzled looks, then dashed away. When they returned in an hour each carried a full bushel of peanuts. Their hands were still dirty from digging peanuts out of the sandy soil. I thanked my helpers, then shooed them off.

Behind locked doors I began my work or rather our work. I knew my hands were guided by a force other than my own. God would show me practical ways to use His creation. Carefully, I ground the peanuts into a fine powder. After heating the powder I squeezed it under a hand press. The oil flowed freely into a cup.

Hours of testing paid off in exciting results. I discovered the peanut oil would blend with other fluids easily. It could be broken down to soap, cooking and rubbing oil, margarine, and cosmetics.

"Praise be, my Lord, stay with me and lead my hands!" I exclaimed.

He did just that. From the peanuts came countless surprises. Carefully, I isolated the fats, the sugars, the resins, and starches. I discovered the peanuts contained pentoses, lysin, amino acids—and so many more treasures. Peanuts were so much more than food. The little peanut held so many gifts for people to use. Now the businessmen must see its worth.

Days and nights slipped away as I worked. By heating and mixing, my peanut chemicals showed their true value. They could be used for inks, candy, flour, shoe polish, salve, dyes—even shaving cream!

"Surely, You have outdone Yourself!" I shouted to my Partner in the lab. Yet my fingers could not stop. On and on my hands worked.

By adding water to the peanut powder, then heating and stirring it, a tasty creamy milk resulted. I guzzled a glassful eagerly.

From the red skin of the peanut, I discovered a fine quality paper could be made. The peanut hulls could be used as a soil conditioner.

I lost all thoughts of time. Finally I staggered from the lab. One of the students who had been in the hallway earlier rushed to my side.

"Dr. Carver—are you all right? You've been working in there for six days and six nights. Why wouldn't you answer the door?"

I smiled, resting a weary arm on my friend's shoulder. "We had much to do," I answered. "But now we will be able to use every peanut we have raised. Harvest each and every peanut crop. We can use peanuts to wash with, to drink, to rub on our bodies—for just about anything. We have found the answer."

"We?" the student asked, shaking his head. "But you were alone in the lab, weren't you?"

"Oh, no," I replied. "I was not alone for a moment."

Big Decisions

Once again the people in the South were happy. Who would have thought that tiny peanuts could bring such big smiles and joyful laughter? Now people had no trouble selling their peanuts. The new uses for peanuts gave birth to shelling and crushing mills across the Southland. In city factories and on country farms, jobs increased. In my classroom and lab I turned my attention to the sweet potato. Like the peanut, it held untold mysteries. Before long, I had discovered the sweet potato could furnish flour, ink, starch, tapioca, and dyes. What fun the Lord must have had wrapping treasures in such unusual packages for people to discover.

But in the midst of our joy came sorrow.

One afternoon I was inspecting our "school on wheels." The horses which had pulled our classroom across the countryside had been replaced by a hearty engine. As I listened to the engine's steady chugging, a young boy dashed up to me. Without speaking he thrust a note into my hand. I noticed the lad's tear-filled eyes and pursed mouth. Before I could speak, he was gone. As I opened the paper my whole body tensed. The message was brief.

Dr. Washington died this morning.

Dr. Washington—dead *at only fifty-six*. The words sank in slowly. True, he had seemed tired after a fund-raising trip up North. His voice sounded weak and his face drawn. But all of us thought days of rest at Tuskegee would rebuild his strength as it had before.

And now he was gone. Our Savior had called a worthy servant to His side.

Alone I walked across the campus like Dr. Washington and I had done so often. The brick buildings seemed so much taller. What powerful testimony they gave to my friend's life as they stood silently in the afternoon sunlight.

Gone. Booker T. Washington was gone. And as I returned to my room early that evening, I wondered if maybe it was time for me to leave Tuskegee also. Were there not younger teachers with new ideas who should be leading students? Perhaps I had stayed at Tuskegee long enough.

I slept uneasily that night, wrestling with the decision. I prayed for the Lord to guide my direction.

A former United States president helped me make my decision.

For as long as I could remember, Theodore Roosevelt had been a friend to both Dr. Washington and Tuskegee. The death of Dr. Washington brought the noted American to the funeral. His words offered us comfort.

"Dr. Washington spent his life bettering the world for his black people," the former president told those who had gathered for a luncheon after the funeral ceremony. "In doing this, he made a better life for all people everywhere."

I waited until our distinguished guest was seated by himself in a corner chair. He was a large man, his face reddened by outdoor adventures. He smiled as I approached and took a seat close by. I felt the need to share my thoughts of leaving Tuskegee with someone else. As I revealed my thinking to Mr. Roosevelt, he seemed suddenly excited. His tea-cup clattered in his hand until he set it on a nearby table. Smoothing his short moustache with two fingers, he leaned close to me.

"You—leave Tuskegee?" he said. "But with Dr. Washington gone . . ."

I nodded. "That is the reason. He is the one who brought me here, and perhaps it is time I move on so that the changes may be complete."

"Do they pay you well here?" Mr. Roosevelt asked.

I chuckled and nodded. The school treasurer at Tuskegee often became angry with me for not cashing my paychecks. Usually, I just tucked them inside a book or in my dresser drawer. I had little need for money.

"I am comfortable," I answered. "It is just that— that perhaps a person can remain in one place too long."

As Mr. Roosevelt sat back in his chair, a wide smile crossed his face. "My dear friend," he said, "I have traveled in countries all over the world. I could not begin to tell you how many people know of this school, of the work President Washington and you have done. Your discoveries have helped the native farmers in the Congo and the ranch farmers in South America. The graduates of your school cover the world, sharing your ideas and methods."

Mr. Roosevelt leaned forward resting his own hand on mine.

"We have lost our leader at Tuskegee—a good friend to us both. But you must remain. There is no more important work than what you are doing."

The words from this kind man mingled with the thoughts inside of me. I knew at that moment that the Lord was telling me the same thing. I had no peace about leaving. The decision was made. I would stay on at Tuskegee. A calmness from the Lord confirmed my decision.

My duties allowed me more and more time in my laboratory. But I made sure much of my time was spent with the students. One of my greatest pleasures was my own "Bible Class."

It all started quite by accident. Now and then a few students would stop by my room on Sunday evening. Usually the students had questions arising from the church service they had attended that day.

"It's just that sometimes the Lord's world and the world of science seem divided," one thin lad told me. "How do you, or rather *can* you, bring them both together?"

"No one needs to bring them together," I answered, eager to accept the challenge. "Everything we have in our world of science springs from the world God has created for us. Take nature, for instance." I pulled the flower from my lapel. "This

blossom came from a seed which was created so many years ago. It has survived floods, tornadoes, and all the attacks of man. Now it shares its beauty with us. Soon it will again bear the seed which will continue the cycle of life. It is God's creation, His way of things. Science is simply a study of God's creations."

The hours slipped by quickly during our talks about God and the Bible. I was grateful I had studied the Good Book in my youth. Often I was asked my own opinions, based on what I thought the Lord's way to be. The students asked every imaginable question—and a few more!

"Professor Carver, what do you think God would say about cigarettes?" one young man asked. "Would He approve of smoking?"

I rubbed my chin slowly. "It seems to me," I answered, "if God had intended the human nose to be used for a chimney, He would have turned our nostrils up." Laughter clattered across the room.

Another student spoke, "I have a hard time starting each day. Is there a special secret to beginning every day in your life?"

"So often we ask the Lord to help us fulfill our goals. Have you ever thought about asking Him what we might do to help Him?"

As I looked at the students gathered in my room, I could tell the idea was a fresh one.

"As for my own way of beginning each day, you know there is a small grove of trees behind this building. One tree has been cut down, leaving a little stump. Each morning at four o'clock when I arise, I go out and sit on that stump. I ask the good Lord what I am to do each day. Then I go ahead and do it."

"You get up at four o'clock every morning!" one student blurted out. "I could never get up that early!"

I chuckled. "Don't worry, my friend. The Lord talks to late risers, too."

The talk sessions brought me special joy. But soon the students filled my room on Sunday evenings. We had to find a new place to meet, and I was told we could use the assembly room in the Carnegie Library.

"But we will not need that large a place," I told the Tuskegee officials. "There are three hundred seats in that room."

"Maybe you won't need such a big place," was the answer, "but try it for a while."

I was proven wrong. Each Sunday evening the students crowded into the assembly room. How eagerly our students sought the Lord's Word.

One morning while I was preparing a lesson from Genesis, the mailman brought another speaking request. The United Peanut Growers Association was meeting in Montgomery, Alabama. It was their very first meeting, and they wanted me to be their guest of honor.

Speaking in public had never been among my favorite pleasures. It was one thing talking before a gathering of Tuskegee students—they were like family. But this would be a collection of strangers.

Yet the invitation was an opportunity to thank these people for the work they had done. I sent my acceptance letter and prepared for the trip.

It was a hot September morning when I boarded the train for Montgomery. My suitcase was heavy—filled with specimen jars of peanut extracts. The Jim-Crow cars were crowded with my people, and some looked at my stuffed bag with curiosity. The white folks in the cars ahead paid little mind to me.

Upon my arrival in Montgomery, I hurried to the hotel. I was scheduled to speak in fifteen minutes. Before I could go inside the lobby, the doorman blocked my way.

"What do you want?" he snapped.

I rested my suitcase on the ground and wiped the sweat from my head with a handkerchief.

"I have been invited to speak before the United Peanut Growers Association. The delegates will be waiting."

The doorman shook his head. "No niggers are allowed here. Move on!"

"But I have a letter from the president of the association," I protested, fumbling inside my coat. "Here is the letter. You can read it for yourself."

"Don't tell me what to do, nigger. You are not coming in this hotel." The doorman turned and walked away.

What should I do? Had I traveled all this way to simply return home? For a moment I stood thinking about what to do.

The sight of a bellboy helped make up my mind. I motioned him over, wrote a quick note on the back of the envelope, and sent him to the meeting.

A few minutes later the bellboy returned. "Come with me," he said. Together we went to the back of the hotel, entered a rear door, then rode the freight elevator up to the proper floor.

I was just being introduced when I arrived at the meeting room. Opening my bag on the speaker's table, I presented my talk. When I had finished, the delegates' kind words made me glad I had come.

"Peanuts have helped rebuild the South," one delegate told me. "Thank you for coming. We hope you will be willing to help us again."

That opportunity to help came sooner than I expected. In January of 1921, I was invited to Washington, D.C. The Senate Ways and Means Committee in Congress was studying an important tariff bill. This bill, if made law, would help the peanut farmers in America.

For many years peanuts had been brought into America from other countries. The tax on the imported peanuts was only half a cent a pound.

"We cannot raise peanuts in America if they can be brought in so cheaply," the peanut growers told me. "Please go to Washington for us. Tell them to raise the tariff. Then we can compete with the foreign growers.

"I know nothing about tariffs and bills," I admitted.

"But no one knows more about the peanut. Please, Professor Carver."

It was a plea I could not refuse. I packed my suitcase again and left for Washington.

The Washington train station was the busiest place I had ever seen. People scurried everywhere to the sound of hissing engines and blaring whistles. Since I was carrying a large wooden case in addition to my traveling bag, I hoped someone might meet me. No one appeared so I made my way outside and hailed a taxicab.

"Where you headed, Mister?"

As I slid into the back seat, I was grateful to rid myself of the weight of the wooden case and my

traveling bag. The trip from Tuskegee had been a long one. Sitting up all night in a crowded, smoke-filled railroad car had not been pleasant.

"Please just drive me around the city," I answered.

The driver shook his head. "Not before I see some money, Mister. Sightseein' trips is three bucks an hour, in advance.

Awkwardly, I withdrew the money from a change purse. The wooden case, traveling bag, and my own lanky frame offered little extra space in the back seat of the car.

"Any place special you want to see?" the driver asked. "Maybe the Washington Monument, the White House, Lincoln's . . ."

"Perhaps the Zoological Park would be a good place to start," I replied. "And the young cherry trees from Japan would be nice."

Confused and surprised, my driving friend again

shook his head. "Hey, Mister, this is January. I hope you don't expect to see every tree in full bloom."

"No, trees are beautiful any time of the year. Please, just drive."

The minutes rolled swiftly by as we rode up and down the avenues of Washington. I was impressed by the stone buildings on every street. Here and there fresh blades of grass poked their heads through the deep rich soil, contrasting with the small patches of dirty snow on the ground.

Soon it was time for me to go to the Capitol building. I did not want to keep the important men waiting. Perhaps I should have brought notes along with my display of bottles in the case. I had refused an offer of the peanut growers back home to buy me a new suit. Now, as I straightened my tie, I wondered if I had made the right decision. I brushed the lint off my old suit.

The taxicab rolled to a stop. It was too late to worry about a new suit now.

"You got business here, Mister?" The tone of my driver's voice revealed disbelief.

"Yes. I have an appointment with a committee of senators."

My answer was a shock to the driver. "You?" he said unconvinced.

I nodded, resting my wooden case and bag on the pavement. "Yes, it is a strange world, isn't it?" He obviously had never delivered a Negro to the Capitol's white steps before.

Slowly I carried my luggage up the many stone stairs of the Capitol building. A guide led me to the right room. Several men sat in front, huddling over wooden tables. All the chairs in the room were taken. People stood along the walls. I joined them.

". . . and I believe we can end these meetings right here and now."

The man sitting at the end of one of the front tables lifted his water glass to his lips. I trembled a moment, fearing I had arrived too late.

"We have one more speaker to hear," another gentlemen said. "Mr. George Washington Carver from Tuskegee Institute."

The man standing next to me leaned closer. "The peanut farmers don't have a chance," he mumbled. "Those senators have already made up their minds."

I stepped forward. "I am George Washington Carver," I shouted. "May I please now speak to you gentlemen?"

I did not wait for an answer. Slowly I shoved forward, maneuvering my wooden case through the people and chairs. A few people laughed at my clumsiness.

"What do you know about the Hawley-Smoot Bill?" one man yelled out.

"Not a thing," I called back. "Do you?"

Laughter echoed off the walls in the great hall. The chairman rapped his gavel on the table. "Order. We'll have order in this room. Mr. Carver, we will give you ten minutes to speak." His voice was sharp and tired.

Ten minutes. What a short time. There was so much to do, so much to say. As I opened my display case, I prayed for the Lord to help me. I knew I could count on Him.

"The United Peanut Growers Association have asked me to tell you about the peanut and its many uses. I come from Tuskegee, Alabama, where I am engaged in agricultural research work. I have given some attention to the peanut and can tell you that it is one of the richest of all products we get from the soil—rich in food value, rich in properties of chemical constituents, and wonderfully rich in possibilities of utilization."

Carefully I pulled the bottles out of my opened case. Then I removed six small boxes, then ten tiny plaques. I glanced over at the men near me.

"If you will be so kind as to move your papers," I said, "I have a few more displays." Eyes widened around me; there were intent stares on the faces. The audience was watching me closely.

"In ten minutes, I shall only be able to demonstrate a few products we have developed from peanuts. This tube contains breakfast food, made from peanuts and sweet potatoes. Not only is this food delicious in flavor, it is wholesome and easily digested."

"Mr. Carver, may I look at it more closely?" one of the senators asked.

"Certainly," I answered. "And if the tube comes back to me with some missing, I will not be the least bit offended."

Encouraged by the round of laughter, I picked up another jar.

"This is ice cream powder made from the peanut. By simply mixing it with water, a rich and delicious ice cream is produced. This next bottle contains a quinine substitute, useful in fighting malaria. I am certain chemists and doctors could find many more uses."

The minutes ticked away quickly—too quickly. Nervously, I kept glancing at the clock on the side wall.

"This collection of bottles contains dyes, each tested and found to hold their color and not to harm the human skin. In this box we have peanut fodder for livestock."

The ten minutes was up. Carefully I began putting my display items away.

"The climate and soil of the South is particularly suited for peanut growing. We must protect this market, our American market."

A voice was heard at one end of the table. "Mr. Chairman, Mr. Carver's time should be extended. This is all too interesting to be cut off."

"Yes!" agreed three other voices. "Agreed! Agreed!" shouted another. The smiling chairman rapped his gavel. "Please, Mr. Carver, continue at your own speed."

Happily I agreed. For the next two hours, I continued to share the secrets of the peanut. Each time I offered to stop, I was persuaded to go on.

"Peanuts can be eaten when meat can't," I said, in closing. "Peanuts are the perfect food. They are always safe."

One of the senators pointed his pencil at me. "Where did you learn all this?"

I answered simply, "From a book."

"What book?" the senator shot back.

I smiled. "The Bible. It says that God has given us everything for our use. He has revealed to me some of the wonders of the fruit of His earth. In the first chapter of Genesis we are told, 'Behold, I have given you every herb bearing seed, which is upon the face of all the earth, and every tree, which is the fruit of a tree yielding seed; to you it shall be for meat.' That's what He means when he uses the word meat. There is everything there to strengthen, nourish and keep the body alive and healthy."

Finally, the men had heard enough. I gathered up my displays. Several of the senators came over to shake my hand.

For an hour I roamed through the Capitol looking at the many statues. It was a thrill to stand where the leaders of the country had made important decisions and speeches.

As I stood, silently gazing at a picture of Abraham Lincoln, a young senator rushed up to me. He grabbed my hand and shook it heartily.

"You did it, Mr. Carver. The peanut is covered in the Hawley-Smoot Tariff Bill. You've won your battle."

I smiled. The Lord had helped me once more. Peanut farmers could grow their crops without fear of being undersold by foreign countries.

Now it was back to Tuskegee. There was still more work to be done.

Twilight

Visitors on the Tuskegee campus were a common sight. Teachers and farming experts came from all over the world to study our agricultural methods and school. Many of these people returned to their countries and opened classrooms for their own students.

But the visitor who sat in my small office that afternoon had come on a special mission. A streak of sunlight sparkled on the large diamond ring on his left hand. The rich gold of his cuff links winked at me.

"I bring you greetings from Thomas Edison," the gentleman said in a crisp voice. "As his secretary, I also bring you an offer. Mr. Edison would like you to join his laboratory staff in New Jersey."

Work for Thomas Edison? For as long as I could remember, this amazing genius had been creating inventions that were changing the world. The phonograph, the microphone, the incandescent lamp, the storage battery—the list seemed endless.

As the secretary spoke, I noticed his fine suit of clothes. The spun threads seemed to glow. Was it cotton? Silk, perhaps. I wondered if husks, properly stretched and spun, could . . .

"Professor Carver, did you hear me?"

I fumbled for words, ashamed at being lost in my own thoughts. "No, I'm sorry. What were you saying?"

The man took a monogrammed handkerchief from his suit pocket. "I was merely repeating Mr. Edison's words which he asked me to relay to you. He said, 'Together we shall unlock the universe. Your limited facilities here delay and hamper you. We can offer you everything with which to work.' That is what Mr. Edison said."

Slowly I scratched my right ear. How I wanted to ask this man about the fabric in his suit.

"And I am prepared to offer you a salary of $100,000 a year," Mr. Edison's secretary continued. "I believe that would be a considerable increase from your present salary."

I chuckled. That was certainly true. Since I had come to Tuskegee in 1896, I had received $1500 each year and I used little of it. Yes, $100,000 was a "considerable increase."

"I have great respect for Mr. Edison," I answered. "I am sorry to refuse his offer."

"Then don't, sir. Think what you could do with a fully-equipped laboratory and the best assistants."

I almost shook my head. "No, I believe I can do my best work here at Tuskegee. I am sixty years old, my dear friend. New gadgets and equipment would only confuse a tired man like me. As for an assistant, I am one myself. I am only God's helper in His little laboratory. But please thank Mr. Edison and wish him well."

It was good to feel appreciated. But I had no desire to leave Tuskegee. It was my home—the people here were my family. I thought of people like Lonny Johnston.

Fourteen-year-old Lonny was the son of the man who tended our farm animals. Always wearing a wide smile, Lonny was a favorite among our Tuskegee staff.

One morning, as I watched Lonny lead two cows to water, I noticed the boy was limping more than usual. Lonny had been kicked by a horse years before, and the ligaments had grown tight in healing. It seemed the boy would be lame all his life. Unless . . .

"Lonny, come over here," I called. "Bring your father, too."

For the next few minutes I talked to Lonny and his father. Their eyes widened as I shared my idea.

"I know you've been using mineral oil on your leg," I said, "but I'm thinking peanut oil might be better. It just might help nourish those damaged muscles. Do you want to give it a try?"

Lonny jumped up. "Can we start now, Mister Carver? Can we?"

"We are most grateful," Lonny's father said, rubbing his hands on his jeans.

We began at once. Each day Lonny came by for a massage. I rubbed the oil in deeply, back and forth. God blessed our efforts. In only six months, Lonny's limp had disappeared.

"I can play baseball!" Lonny exclaimed. "The kids at school even pick me to be on their team."

Lonny's success led me into more experiments with peanut oil. Two worried parents brought their son to me. A handsome and healthy boy, he had fallen victim to infantile paralysis. Through a program of regular massage and exercise, the lad was able to use a cane instead of crutches. In a few more months he was walking without support. Sadly enough, an eager newspaper reporter learned of our success. As I ate breakfast one morning, a friend dropped a newspaper before me. I shuddered as I read the headline:

PEANUT MAN DISCOVERS CURE FOR INFANTILE PARALYSIS

More reporters swarmed to the campus. Parents of stricken children brought them from all over the country.

"My treatment is no cure," I told them all. "Massaging peanut oil into the limbs of the body will not affect the disease itself. The best it can do is restore a bit of life to wasted areas."

No one listened. Telegrams, long distance telephone calls, hundreds of letters arrived each day. Everyone wanted help. My laboratory became a miniature hospital. From morning until night, I rubbed diseased legs and arms. And as I rubbed, I prayed, "Lord, let my humble hands carry Thy healing grace."

One Saturday morning I knelt beside a young girl on a cot. She lay quietly holding her small doll. Slowly, I massaged the girl's thin twisted legs.

"You are a nice man," the girl whispered. "You make my legs feel cool."

I smiled. "If you keep . . ."

Suddenly, the laboratory door banged open. A tall man, his long black hair tousled, ran to the cot and stood looking down at us. The intruder grabbed my sweater.

"I got this bad leg," he shouted. "You're going to fix it."

Frightened, the girl moved back. She gripped her doll tightly.

"You will have to wait your turn," I answered firmly. "Right now I am busy." Again I began rubbing the girl's legs.

"Hey, nigger, don't you turn your back on me!" the stranger snapped. "I drove one hundred miles to see you. Now you look at my leg and take care of it."

Once more the girl drew back in fear. Slowly, I stood up and faced the ill-mannered man.

"Neither my prayers nor the power of this

medicine could penetrate the profanity in your heart," I declared sternly. "I cannot help you because you would rather hate me than be helped. I suggest you go now, and pray for the Lord's forgiveness."

Fire danced in the man's eyes as his lip curled into a vicious sneer. Would he hit me? For a long moment he stood staring. Then he turned and left, banging the door.

"Now, where were we?" I said softly, returning to the girl on the cot. "I remember. You were just going to tell me about your doll."

Once more the girl's eyes brightened as she began to talk. Our angry intruder was quickly forgotten.

Finally, after many months, the commotion died down. We had treated 250 cases of infantile paralysis. All of them had shown some improvement. Many of the boys and girls recovered completely. The National Foundation of Infantile Paralysis awarded Tuskegee money for additional research.

In 1937, I met one of the most interesting men I had ever known. Henry Ford was known to the world as an automobile manufacturer. My friends drove his Model A Fords about campus. But to me, he became a special friend. He was a dreamer, and he worked hard to turn those dreams into reality. Often, he enjoyed visiting the campus and talking with our students.

"Well, Mr. Carver," he would say, "what have you added to this place since the last time I came?"

Always I had something new to show him. By 1940, one hundred buildings dotted our campus. Green, healthy shrubs trimmed walks and pathways.

Above us spreading magnolia blossoms danced in the wind, bowing before towering elm trees. How different it looked now from when I had arrived.

Inside classrooms and laboratories, and outside in the fields, two thousand young men and women exchanged ideas. They were learning to challenge their minds.

As Henry Ford and I walked there was no need for conversation. We enjoyed watching the students at work.

Now and then I traveled north to Michigan. Next to his giant automobile plant, Henry raised vast fields of soybeans. They were his special treasure, as peanuts were mine. A lab was built in the soybean fields where I could work. I developed a soybean plastic which my delighted friend quickly put to use in his automobiles. Few people knew their instrument panels and gearshift knobs had come from fields of soybeans!

But the years were slowing me down. Reluctantly, I took on an assistant at Tuskegee. As I neared my eightieth year, I knew someone else should be ready to complete any tasks I might not be able to finish.

One December morning in 1942, I slipped on a small patch of ice. Such a fuss people made! My assistant, Austin Curtis, insisted I stay in bed and rest. Our favorite Tuskegee cook, Juanita Jones, took me as her special patient. The meals she brought me were better suited for royalty.

I longed to work in my lab, yet my strength did not return. Nevertheless, Austin and Juanita had no intention of letting me waste time. One afternoon the two of them appeared at the doorway to my bedroom. They held their hands behind their backs.

I sat up in bed. "You two look very suspicious," I said. "What are you holding?"

Austin produced a complete set of paints and Juanita carried a small bed table and paper.

"People will be expecting your regular Christmas cards," said Juanita.

"You can start painting them now," Austin added. "Just don't complain about the quality of the paints."

I glanced down at the small bottles. Sure enough, they were paints I had mixed in the laboratory.

Soon I was busy at work. On each card, I wrote the words "Peace on Earth and Good Will to men." I smiled. Yes, that is the world the Lord intended. I prayed that my life and work had helped in a small way to make the world peaceful and make Him happy.

An hour later I set my paints and cards aside. From the table beside the bed, I took the worn Bible Mariah Watkins had given me many years ago. Opening the pages, I began to read Psalm 23: "The Lord is my shepherd; I shall not want . . ."

BIRMINGHAM BANNER
Alabama

Extra!

January 5, 1943   5¢

CARVER DIES

Tuskegee — George Washington Carver, man's slave who became God's scientist, died peacefully in his sleep early this morning.

Dr. George Washington Carver, 79 years old, who was born a slave and became one of the greatest of American scientists, is dead.

He had been in failing health for several years, and last month suffered a fall from which he never recovered. He died Tuesday night in his home on the campus of Tuskegee Institute, where he had taught since 1896. He was confined to his bed for 10 days before his death, which was attributed to heart disease.

Funeral services will be either Thursday or Friday. The body will lie in state at the school until burial in Tuskegee Cemetery near the grave of Booker T. Washington, founder of Tuskegee Institute.

Dr. Carver's chemical discoveries, especially of products made from sweet potatoes and peanuts, increased the income of the South by many millions of dollars. Throughout his life he had preached crop diversification and self-sufficiency, and last year was honored by the Progressive Farmers Association for having contributed the greatest service to Southern agriculture.

HONORED IN BRITAIN

He was appointed collaborator in the Bureau of Plant Industry of the United States Department of Agriculture in August, 1935. He became a member of the Royal Society of Arts, London, in 1917.

BIBLIOGRAPHY

Albus, Harry. *The Peanut Man.* Grand Rapids, Michigan: Wm. B. Eerdmans Publishing Company, 1948.

Bontemps, Arna. *The Story of George Washington Carver.* New York: Grosset & Dunlap, 1954.

Borth, Christy. *Pioneers of Plenty—The Story of Chemurgy.* New York: Bobbs-Merrill, 1942.

Bullock, Ralph W. *In Spite of Handicaps.* New York: Association Press, 1927.

Campbell, Thomas M. *The Movable School Goes to The Negro Farmer.* Alabama: Tuskegee Institute Press, 1926.

Clark, Glenn. *The Man Who Talks With the Flowers.* St. Paul, Minnesota: Macalester Park Publishing Company, 1939.

Coy, Harold. *The Real Book About George Washington Carver.* New York: Garden City Books, 1951.

Epstein, Sam. *George Washington Carver: Negro Scientist.* Champaign, Illinois: Garrard Publishing Company, 1960.

Graham, Shirley and Lipscomb, G. D., *Dr. George Washington Carver, Scientist.* New York: Julian Messner, Inc., 1944.

Holt, Rackam. *George Washington Carver: An American Biography.* New York: Doubleday and Company, 1943.

Jenness, Mary. *The Man Who Asked God Questions—George Washington Carver.* New York: Frontier Books, 1946.

Johnson, F. Roy. *The Peanut Story*. Murfreesboro, North Carolina: Johnson Publishing Company, 1964.

Mathews, Basil. *Booker T. Washington*. Cambridge, Massachusetts: Harvard University Press, 1948.

Means, Florence Crandall. *Carver's George*. Boston, Massachusetts: Houghton Mifflin Company, 1952.

Merritt, Raleigh. *From Captivity to Fame*. Boston, Massachusetts: Meador Publishing Company, 1938.

Richardson, Ben. *Great American Negroes*. New York: Thomas Crowell, 1945.

Smith, Alvin D. *George Washington Carver: Man of God*. New York: Exposition Press, 1954.

Thomas, Henry. *George Washington Carver*. New York: G. P. Putnam's Sons, 1958.

INDEX

SOWERS SERIES